The Difference it Makes

Having Christ in My Life and Your Life

The Difference it Makes
Having Christ in My Life and Your Life

Deborah Woodley

authorHOUSE®

AuthorHouse™
1663 Liberty Drive
Bloomington, IN 47403
www.authorhouse.com
Phone: 1-800-839-8640

First published by AuthorHouse   09/17/2011

ISBN: 978-1-4670-3583-5 (sc)
ISBN: 978-1-4670-3582-8 (ebk)

Library of Congress Control Number: 2011916463

Printed in the United States of America

Contents

<u>Leamon Woodley Jr. and Deborah Woodley</u>

Proud parents of two wonderful children

who God has blessed us to nurture and

raise to believe in Him and honor His word.

Foreword

I found this woman first in my heart prior to physically meeting her. I didn't know how we would meet; however, I knew she would become my wife. Deborah is my companion, my partner for life, my sweetheart, and my best friend. I love the thoughtful things she does to show how much she cares and the joy and happiness she brings me.

As the mother of my children, she is always busy doing something to edify or up-lift someone else while making them feel valued. At the same time, she puts God first in our lives and somehow managed to orchestrate time to serve and give selflessly of herself daily. I cherish the wisdom she obtains from God, the path she has travel with me, the belief and support she gives me and the special pride she inspired in our children. I trust her and she means the world to me.

As you read her book, be encouraged and see the picture of faith and hope through her life journey with Christ. A mighty woman of God with insight and discernment; Deborah knows who she is in Christ. Whether it is a task or a mission she is trying to accomplish, she sees past what is in front of her. Enjoy!

Leamon J. Woodley, Jr.

Leamon J. Woodley, Jr.
US Army Retired, MSG
Washington State Powerlifting Hall of Fame
        Inducted March 5, 2011

Acknowledgements

I would like to thank God the Father, Son, and Holy Spirit for the life He has allowed me to live in order to give Him all the glory, honor and raise. I am thankful for my family and friends, for their support and the love they give in return. I am grateful for my Mother, the late Lillie Bell Rivers, for nurturing me and setting a Godly example of a true woman of God. She has been my foundation. I am grateful for my church families in military Chapels across the globe. They allowed me to lead others as God was leading me in my spiritual walk and calling to serve in the Women's Ministry and other areas. I thank my oldest sister Gloria for her tireless patience, mentorship and strength. To my husband, Leamon Jr., I thank him for his love and friendship. My daughter, Leamona for becoming the independent woman she has become. To my son, Leamon, III, it is a pleasure to be a part his growth and development into a responsible young man. I pray that he will make a difference in society—a difference that will give glory and honor to God. Lastly, I appreciate my friend Virginia Mathews for her expertise in art and graphics along with her encouragement.

Author's Notes

I dedicate this book to everyone who desires to know God on a personal level to include the ones who are unsure if God hears your heart and knows your desires. Allow my true stories to encourage you. If you are hurting, experiencing low self esteem, racism, loneliness, inferiority and thinking you don't know why you are here, this book is for you.

You have everything in life and all your material and physical needs are fulfilled and peace of mind is absent from your life, I contribute this book to you. Stress and no rest are hazardous to your health and God knows what is best for you.

If you believe that Jesus Christ is Lord and the Son of God and have not accepted him as your Lord and Savior by confession with your mouth from your heart, I recommend you do so immediately while reading this book. Then, I pray that you get into a bible base teaching church and get plugged in—to obtain assistance in your spiritual growth through fellowshipping and learning amongst believers. Further, have fun, and know that having Christ in your Life will make a difference in failure or success, peace during trials and tribulation, hope in the middle of uncontrolled circumstances and direction when you don't know which way to turn. This book will make you laugh and cry, but most of all, it will enlighten you on how much He loves you and want to be your Father in Heaven and on earth.

Deborah Woodley

Deborah Woodley
US Army Retiree, SFC
Motivational Speaker
Women Ministry Leader

Introduction

I am a Southern girl from the projects of Chattanooga, Tennessee.

I was raised by a special woman who would become a widow. Her name is Lillie Bell Rivers. She knew the meaning of struggle; living on government assistance and medical aid when it was needed. I had the best of everything because my mother not only had a relationship with Christ; she walked the talk in her everyday life.

As a student, I had perfect attendance in grades sixth through 12th. I had to work harder than some kids just to be an average student. So, in January of 1979 at the age of 17 years, I joined the military. Although I believed in myself and felt that I was someone special, I wanted to prove to myself that I could be a productive citizen. My goal was to one day give back to my community.

I consider myself blessed.

I have walked in the favor of God in a number of areas of my life. First, my husband and I are dual military retirees with a combination of 47 years of serving and 30 years of marriage. Secondly, I know it had the grace of God on my life, because there were a couple of times when I made decisions that could have led me to prison. God spared me from the agony of having my children who would have been left behind for someone else to care for. Third, I chose to be a positive force in the earth. I could have chosen to be bitter which would have led me to deal with the negative health side effects that bitterness brings. Fourth, I chose to love Jesus. The alternative, which is the worst of all the things that could have befallen me, is that I could have lived in a place where I did not have the freedom to learn about Jesus Christ. He is my Lord and Savior, who truly makes the difference in everything I think or do. Life can be a hit and miss game with no way out of the foulness that can crop up in one's mind. Yet, as Christians, we have to be taught how to overcome. We have to practice it and walk it out by Faith.

Sometimes, we have to do it alone and trust totally in God to see us through. When God gives us a vision, He gives provision also. When we find ourselves being tempted, the Holy Spirit will give us an escape route to choose. God will let us see from this point, that we do have an option.

If you don't know what I am talking about, read further. As you go on my Faith Journey, you will see that there were times of confusion, uncontrolled circumstances and decisions that were made from my heart, while I trusted God to take care of me whether it was consciously or unconsciously.

Grace and Favor

Wow, I am living a life that demonstrates the difference it makes having Christ in my life. I feel an urgency to share my story, because being a Christian means you have to walk the talk in the world in grace and humility, while setting an example for your family, friends and community. I was bullied in elementary school and made a decision not to take it anymore. I showed my assailant the tool I would use to knock off his head and gave him a choice whether he would continue the abuse. He thought I was crazy, but after that, he left me alone. I didn't want to do it, but I was afraid of him and at the same time, deep down, I liked him too. I am not telling anyone to respond with violence when bullied, but I am sharing what worked for me during a particular time period in my life. I had a chance, later as a teenager, to explain to him how afraid I was of him. I told him that I did not have it in my heart to hurt him, but I wasn't going to be pushed around any longer.

Integration to a multicultural middle school, East Side Junior High School, was the beginning of the change that I yearned. I chose to attend a blended race high school, Brainerd High School across town instead of Howard High School which was across the street from our apartment in the Maurice Poss Homes Projects. This was my own decision. My mother allowed me to branch out in my vision for my young life in the 70s. I also thank God for Dr. Martin Luther King, Jr., who I know made a difference in my life too through the anointing power of God which dwelled upon his life. He had a dream to see little black and white boys and girls being educated side my side.

I understand now that God worked his plan through Grace and Favor through the trials and tribulations of Martin Luther King, Jr. When my Class of 1979 had its first class reunion, I made sure I mentioned to a couple of classmates, that it was God who allowed me to have perfect attendance from sixth through twelfth grade and in the US Army thus far. I remembered the class leaders meant it to be a joke by announcing that I had perfect attendance from sixth to twelfth grade with an average grade point average (GPA) then everyone laughed. I smiled because it was true with a lot of history behind it on why I did the things I did. Wow! What a difference it made having Christ in my mother's life because she was able to trust God for my life too without holding me back or keeping me in a box. Because my mother trusted God to guide me, it seemed, I was the only child in my community who was always looking for a way to move away or get away and start anything new.

I joined the US Army on paper in January 1979, 10 months before my eighteenth birthday and I kept it a secret from other family and friends for a reason. I knew I needed to make this transition deep inside me, and distractions were not an option for me to entertain because I had an urgency to move. After graduation in June, I worked around town during the summer months then I departed to the US Army. I was stationed at Fort Jackson in South Carolina (Paradise Island) that September. I turned 18 years old shortly after arriving for active duty. I had no fear of being me in any and every situation, while standing up for what was right as I became educated in the basic operations of being a soldier. I was having fun, because I knew God set a system of government in place, just for me, so I could be treated fairly. I made sure that I read and understood all the regulations pertaining to promotion, as well as the protocols regarding how to serve soldiers in an administrative capacity. I wasn't looking for a husband when I arrived at Fort Bragg in North Carolina, but a man name Leamon was looking for a wife. He somehow knew that I would be his wife prior to ever meeting me. Years later, I found this out when he spoke on the phone to a high school friend of mine, the late Reggie White. Reggie asked Leamon how we met and Leamon told him that he observed me daily in our dining facility on the military base. He said, he knew in his heart that I would become his wife. Amazingly, circumstances allowed us to meet when I was at a party with other soldiers. I had a friend named Pat, who was always looking out for me. I was a young, adventurous female soldier, who was learning how to be a woman at the same time. Pat wanted to ensure I would get back to the barracks safely, so she asked the DJ to take me back to base. To my surprise, the DJ was Leamon. He was calm, well dressed and reserved. He was honored to take me home and he was nice and didn't try to make a pass at me. He rarely said a word other than asking me where I was from and basic information. I felt he was watching me dance a lot at the party on the dance floor, but he showed no interest in me personally. He did not talk much, just observed me and later he became my friend. I had no idea of his motives to date me. He made himself available to always assist me when I needed someone. Leamon Jr., was getting to know me as we started to spend time together.

Circumstances happened in the barracks that allowed him the opportunity to step up to the plate in being a true friend. By this time, I realized that he would be there for me when I got in trouble and when I needed someone to help me stay strong and endure the growth process of being a young soldier. Every time I needed someone to count on and be reliable for me, Leamon Jr. was always available for me and ready to take me wherever I needed to go away from the barracks. When I needed someone to talk to, he was a listener. I thought I would date another interested soldier, but sometimes in life, what we want is not always good for us. Only through living out the consequences of our decisions, we soon learn what is better for us. Operating in wisdom from God is protection. I learned that a huge amount of negative consequences can be prevented, if we listen to God's voice through His word and take head to the guidance of the Holy Spirit. It is amazingly how He ministers to our very soul when we pray to Him for understanding.

Occasionally, I informed Leamon about my sponsor harassing me or bullying me in the barracks. This girl was assigned to support me when I arrived at Fort Bragg, but she gave me every reason to believe I was being recruited into a lesbianism lifestyle. During the late 70s, we did not have rooms in our barracks that we could secure our living space. It was an open bay with partitions dividing the personal sleeping space from other female soldiers. A couple of females with higher rank lived in secure rooms with locks on their doors. I felt as though I was being harassed because I did not want to participate with my sponsor's and her other girl friends outings. My sponsor's sleeping space was next to mine. She would do little things to lure me into her space. As a result, I was persuaded to resist her friendship and her advances whenever she communicated with me. All the females in the barracks had to attend a GI Party. This was not the typical party where you go listen to music and dance and get your groove on. It was a cleaning party where everyone was assigned to a small group that would be given a special area to clean and make sure that it was extra spotless.

Again, my sponsor used her rank to control the area where I was assigned to work. She made sure that I was with her in the secluded bathroom cleaning the toilets. I was on the floor using a little toothbrush-type cleaning tool (the kind that you see on television when soldiers are cleaning the toilets). I was thinking and minding my own business. And, while I was down on my hands and knees on the floor cleaning a toilet; she entered my personal space and straddled my body. I came up swinging with body blows. I eventually made it to her torso area as I was in route to her head. I didn't know it, but I lost it. I gave her a beat down that I would later regret. I had built up so much anger at her for harassing me with small things that I took out all of my frustrations at this moment. This was a big thing to me. She was trying to escape the bathroom, but I managed to leach onto her like a bull-dog. By this time, we were in the hallway where everyone could see us. I was the only one throwing punches. I started to think about how there were certain girls who received all of the attention and privileges. I remembered how I had to work twice as hard to stand out during inspections and while doing my job just be noticed. This kept me angry enough to keep fighting her.

Our Barrack's Sergeant came out to see what was going on and I was in a rage. This beautiful black woman with high hopes and dreams was in a frenzy. No one else attempted to break us up because we were now the entertainment and they were laughing. It was no secret that my sponsor was recruiting women to her lifestyle. I knew that I was in trouble after my first sergeant, who was white; asked the military police to also contact my commander. Okay, the word was out, I had assaulted a higher ranking female soldier and I was going to fry. I still had no fear, but I was beginning to believe that I may be in trouble. I just had no idea how much.

Charles D. Ford was my commander during this time in my career. When it was time to see him and we were alone in his office, he said that he had heard the alleged female victim's testimony of my attack. My commander was about to read me my Article 15 for "Assault with Daring Consequences," when he paused and stared at me for a while. I didn't know what he was thinking. At that point, I knew my fate was in his hands. Unexpected, he ask me a question that I will take to my grave; "If you had an opportunity to do this all over again, what would you have done?" Without hesitating, I responded, "Sir, If I had known you were going to send me to a military confinement, I would have killed her because I had every reason to believe that she and her lesbian girls were recruiting me to be in their group." I further explained what was going on. My commander became concern and asked me why I didn't tell anyone.

You see, back then, if you made an accusation against someone for harassment, you better have proof and people to back you up as witnesses. Our barracks housed several females who were assigned to different companies. The barrack's Sergeant was just in charge of clean up rosters, and not personally in charge of us girls. We didn't have our supervisors checking us out on a regular basis to see how we lived. I remember it as if it were yesterday. I had to explain by saying; "They sent me a message that they will give me a blanket party". Then he ask, "Who is going to do this to you", I said, "her girls". A blanket party is when someone gets you down on the floor, throws a blanket on top of you while several others stand or sit on the blanket and beat you up. You cannot defend yourself this way because you are trapped and motionless. These acts happened sometimes back in the late 1970's. They would use brass knuckles to beat you because they cause injury to your body by penetrating the blanket without damaging the perpetrator's knuckles. Some soldiers carried these medals or brass items in case they got into a fight. So, I said, "Sir, I have no way to secure my sleeping space because we only have partitions for privacy in the barracks." I further explained that I could not sleep thinking of them coming to get me because when you mess with one of their girls, you have to mess with all of them. By this time, I was just being honest about how I had come to think about the situation.

My commander said something to me that rings in my ears to this very day. "What I'm about to do, you will never forget, but I will. He tore up that Article 15. This is a form used to initiate legal actions against soldiers who break the laws of the Military Code of Uniform Justice. The punishment that comes with this legal action can include soldiers getting a reduction in rank, or losing a specific amount of money for months or it can include military confinement. This form, everyone knew had power and influence over your military career, if you messed up. Everyone desired to move up in the ranks, so they could be in charge of soldiers and lead. This was the life in the military. Through a process of training and dedication, you will, one day, be able to handle more responsibility. Rank advancements also required the Army to pay you more money as you climbed the ladder of ranks. When my commander tore up the Article 15, I just looked at him with tears in my eyes not knowing what to say. For my personal protection, he gave me 72 hours to move out the barracks. I knew it was the Grace of God on my life. For me to walk out of my commander's office with another chance to pursue my military career, it was a miracle. It was like an out-of-body experience, as I walked back to my barracks. As I walked, I heard a strong voice say, "Call your friend."

There was another incident that occurred during the time I resided in the barracks. This incident and the lifting of the Article 15 influenced my decision to move off base. This is what happened: another girl who I will call Cheryl, whose partition was on the opposite side of mine in the barracks, was conducting strange rituals and practiced Voo-Doo. I never got in her way because I thought: 'to each his own.' I did not socialize with her, because I didn't understand her. I never felt threatened by her, because I was a Christian and stood my grounds in how I was raised. I didn't allow myself to get into religious confrontational conversations with people, because I was satisfied with where I was as a Christian. I never felt it necessary to challenge other religions because I felt that if Christianity worked for my mother, it would work for me. I honestly believed Christianity was the right way and that I was created to praise and worship my Lord and Savior Jesus Christ. I don't remember the exact words that Cheryl spoke, because it was not spoken in correct English. The dialect she used sounded like the words I had heard spoken on television when people were doing witchcraft rituals. I responded in a loud voice, "I don't know what you are saying, but whatever you just put on me is reversed back to you in one hundred fold, in Jesus Name!" I laughed it off, but Cheryl became very angry with me. Then, she painted the partition, which was next to my side of the room, black. I never thought anything else about this craziness. I prayed often thanking God for protecting me like He always did and helping me to do the right thing and be all I could be in the Army.

One day, an ambulance was at our barracks and Cheryl was being carried out. She was screaming at the top of her voice. They had her strapped to the bed. She was using profanity as I walk up. Although I wanted her to feel better, she hated me. I don't know what I ever did to her because I was the youngest in the barracks at that time. I came up to my living space and noticed that people were cleaning up some black liquid tar like substance off the floor. I ask, "My God, what is that?" The barracks Sergeant said, "Cheryl took sick and vomit up from her stomach a black or dark liquid then she became very ill so I called 911." I remember lying in my bed, and the Holy Spirit brought to my attention to always trust in Him and not people and circumstances. I felt my heart saying to God, 'You've got that right!' Life was always exciting for me early in my military career. I was happy that I was still free, out on my own and living it up. Although, I was always close to danger, I was never fearful. Again, God had protected me.

You can understand why, when I heard the voice of God in my soul say; "CALL YOUR FRIEND," that I obeyed. Although, I did not care for him in the same way that he cared for me, at that time, I did just as I was instructed by the Holy Spirit. I went and found my friend; Leamon who I knew cared a lot for me. He took me in his car to Pat's house and kept me there for a couple of weeks. Then on our military payday, he pawned his stereo equipment; the same equipment that he used as a DJ, so we could afford to reside in a trailer off post. God had already prepared Leamon's heart to love me, no matter what. In God's word, it says, *"When a Man finds a wife, he finds a good thing."*

He did not hesitate nor did he put much thought into it. He seemed to know what he needed to do to assist me. Here I was, shacking with a man that I wasn't sure about . . . but he was reliable. He made sure I made it back to base for formations and special duty. I was a good girl friend and cooked for him every day. He did not have to tell me he loved me, because his actions spoke louder than words. I began to care a lot about this young man because he was my best friend and an angel sent from above.

I was fortunate that I did not have to suffer the consequences of my actions. Somehow, I managed to continue my military service; and by the Grace of God with a clean record. I was not allowed to discuss this case with anyone. In some other shape or form, I would have to go back and see the commander who could have initiated that Article 15. Yet, in m y heart, I felt grateful and appreciative that God made a way for me out of a situation that I had gotten myself into. I was full of anger and resentment because of the peer pressure from my female sponsor. I had expected a different outcome. Because she was the first soldier to welcome me to Fort Bragg, I thought she would support me. I was sadly mistaken.

After the incident, I did everything possible to stand out as a good soldier. I called cadence when we ran around post and rock with a sound of soulful singing that made soldiers from all walks of life repeat after me as we jogged in unison. I went to the next level of leadership schooling, Primary Leadership Development Course for 6 weeks (PLDC). By then, my sponsor noticed that that I was still moving forward. She saw that I was advancing in responsibility and rank. She realized that I did not get punished for fighting with her. The word got out—I was dead meat. There was no way that they would confront my commander on his decision. About six months later, it was obvious that nothing had happened to me. I received a promotion to Specialist (SPC). Maybe, my commander, Captain Ford knew of more tragic circumstances around these types of situations that women did in the military. He seemed that he was in the military for a long time and appeared to be around 40 to 50 years of age. I believe that he was an angel, who God used to give me another chance—a chance that I did not deserve. I was happy-go-lucky and very careful in my communications with people. I worked in a Personnel Administrative Office (PAC) for the first 4 years of my military career.

I resided with my best friend for over a year. I began to realize that I was playing the role of a wife without the benefits. I was just rolling with the punches and living good off post, away from threats and influences that could cause me to negatively respond and get into trouble. I began to pay attention to how I was living and compared it to the way that I was raised. Because I was brought up in the church, living together wasn't my idea of righteous living. The fact was I had strayed from the biblical lifestyle that the World's Greatest Mother, Lillie Bell Rivers, had set before me. She was a great role model and it was evident through her actions and the love she used to nurture me and my five siblings. When she visited us, she did not scold me for shacking with Leamon, she was relieved that I was with someone who would be my best friend and look after her baby girl. She came in on the Greyhound Bus to check on her daughter and she stayed a week with us. Leamon still did not talk much, but his love and patience was strong for me and his respect for her was awesome. When she was getting ready to leave and return to Chattanooga, she said, "Leamon will one day be your husband; and he will never leave you." This was a true prophesy. Over the years, I have given him many reasons to leave, but he has stood by my side. I remember smiling at her and I told her that I did not love him like that to marry him.

Little did I know, at the time of Mother's visit, that she was taking nerve pills. She had been worrying about me being so far away from home. I was the only child who left the city, for an adventure. I was the only child living in this big world outside of the Chattanooga-area. I was just enjoying my military life and the freedom of residing off base near Fort Bragg in North Carolina. When I left home for basic training, I wrote and called her a lot, but when I got to permanent party (my first assigned duty station), the pace sped up. Life was hectic and I was going through the challenges of barracks life and adapting to military life. I forgot to contact mom. I got a Red Cross message to contact home. During the time I was going through circumstances in the barracks, Mother was praying a lot for me and she didn't know how to contact me other than going through emergency procedures. My praying mother made a world of difference whether I succeeded or failed in my endeavors. There were so many distractions in this world to knock me off track in pursuing my goals and dreams. Turning 50 years old this year is a blessing. I am able to serve God for the rest of my life without compromising. I learned that if I put God first, everything else falls into place for me mentally, physically and spiritually.

People knew that Leamon Jr. loved me because he let me drive his Dodge Dart when I wanted. No one drove this car but him, and today he still drives that car over 32 years later. In the 70s and 80s, it was a beautiful black car with a white strip on each side, and he wipes it off every chance he gets. It is now a classic that he drives on sunny days only. Yes! We do get a lot of sunny days in Washington State.

I learned that Leamon Jr. liked to watch wrestling on TV, I thought that I would jump on his body and try some of those wrestling moves. At first it was fun, until he pinned me down and I couldn't get loose. I got angry and emotional. I had to apologize to him because I wanted to get anything and knock him up side his head. I had issues that surfaced and I forgot we were playing and I started the rough activity. You see when there is baggage in your life of not trusting men to be there for you, it tends to surface in your current relationships. I remember saying to him that a man did not raise me and none will put their hands on me, period! He looked at me like I was crazy. Later, I realized, at the young age of 18 that I had a problem and did not feel I was marriage material. I prayed. I believed that God would take care of me no matter what; therefore, I kept doing what I could daily as a young soldier girl.

A year went by of living together, and after my 19th birthday, I realized that something was missing. I had started to make rank advancement in the military, by the grace of God. I knew I needed to approach this issue of shacking with my boyfriend. I didn't want to sound like I needed him forever, but I have this desire to live right with God one day. Tomorrow is not promised to us, but I lived like it was for me during this time in my life. I had no peace in my heart the longer I did not approached this issue. I was waiting on a proposal down on one knee like they do on TV. I had no idea that he wanted to marry me, but I knew he was over the hills in love with me. You see, I could not understand love from a man because I had no father figure in my home to share that part of growing up with. I finally mentioned it later that month of our one year anniversary of shacking. He knew we would marry, but I did not consider myself to be a wife. I knew I was a beautiful woman and sometimes while working in this Headquarters Personnel Center in a unit under 189th Maintenance Battalion on Fort Bragg, I carried myself like I owned the world.

When I mentioned that I could no longer shack up with him and play a wife's role, he said, "good, we will marry on our two year mark of living together." We left this conversation at that for about six months. Then we both started to plan how we would do it, but could not afford a big wedding. This did not matter to us as much as it did to be married. We knew that the Army system would reassign one of us soon as we wanted to stay together. During this time, a lot of couples began to get married anyway they could. When Leamon Jr. and I met, we both were new to the base. This was my first permanent party station and it was his second duty station on active duty. He came in from West Germany to Fort Bragg a couple of months prior to my arrival. We had a lot in common: We were both from low income families and wanted to retire from the military. He was conservative and I was an extravert. This was enough for me because there was a balance in characters. I had nowhere else I wanted to be other than serving on active duty with my best friend because it gave me a sense of belonging in a world where I could excel in leadership fairly. We made an appointment at a popular place to marry, south of the Boarder in South Carolina. There was a chapel there. We don't remember the person who executed our wedding vows, but we had friends there with us. This was good enough for us and they are still our friends 30 years later.

Sure enough, months later, we came down on orders for a Permanent Change of Station (PCS) to Germany. I was excited that we were together and I was going again, but this time out of the country. We both were stationed together on Finthen Army Air-Field. We traveled all over everywhere possible. My entire career of 21 years of active duty, we were always stationed together, and I believe it was because of my mother's prayers to God to keep us together. The Grace of God was all over us as a couple because we worked with people from all around the globe. Through difficult and tough times, we made it through. Again, I was the extraverted one and Leamon Jr. was the introverted one to this day. The Favor of God is still on our lives as we season in age. We have attained several acquaintances and a few real friends who are still a part of our lives today.

It was challenging for my sisters because they worked hard to raise their kids. They both had to get the law involved through the courts to get child support for their children. Back then, they only had Welfare and Food Stamps to assist the low income parents who lived in the projects. Both of my sisters were proud and work very diligently to not live in the projects long. They eventually moved out and started renting older affordable houses and apartments that gave them a peace that they were living and working hard to take care of their children. My oldest sister is a great cook and has given her talents and service to employers for over 45 years by cooking in kitchens. She is known as a great cook by many, especially, her family. I will express more about Gloria's recipes in another book. Their life was a living example for me on how not to have kids so fast. I believe that you have to have control over your finances and be able to handle the expenses of taking care of children without a father just in case.

Gloria Jean Hill is precious to me and I love her very much. She single-handed raised 5 children while working hard and long hours continually. I respect her strength, love for me and our family. Her endurance to press through difficult challenges mentally and physically influenced me to plan my life careful.

Mom set the example for us to love one another and keep our families together.

Observation

After Leamon and I got married at the Justice of the Peace Chapel in Dillon, South Carolina, we came back to our trailer to celebrate and party with our friends. Neither of our families was invited to participate in these festivities. I don't remember why they weren't invited, but we fully understood that this relationship was about us together forever and not our family. We could not afford to invite them anyway. We knew we could not afford a wedding, so we were content to wear Pin Strips suites and get married before a judge and a select few soldiers, who were our friends. Our parents never met one another and my mother went to be with our Lord and Savior, Jesus Christ in July 1999. It was never a negative situation; they just lived in two different places, Tennessee and North Carolina. We traveled to many places on vacations around the world and never initiated their connections. We visited them off and on down through the years and we seemed content with this process. Time was vital doing our active duty years of serving our country. We spent time serving in West Germany. There we meet awesome people from all walks of life and they loved us. We noticed that many of our friends had divorced as we ventured in our careers around the world. We were on a mission to complete the task of our military careers together. Although, I had this idea of retiring, I had to trust God. This was a day-by-day trusting Him, because the dangers of military life meant that I could have been dead and gone, on several occasions.

My husband and I came down on orders together to be reassigned overseas to Europe. We travel to Mallorca and Spain; Paris, France. We were on the same ocean in about 1984 on our way to Sweden, when a ship was hijacked and a soldier in a wheel chair was thrown overboard from that ship. Wow! This could have been our ship. We knew we were blessed to be vacationing during that time, but we did not think about it much because danger was always around us in different countries. From 1983-1986, I had grown a lot as a woman and wife from mistakes that could have cause me my life, let alone my marriage. We got back in the United States to serve at Fort Lewis, Washington and I knew it was time to stop taking pregnancy prevention measures and to allow our first born child, Leamona to come into the world. Once again, my mother came to us on the Greyhound Bus on a five day journey across the United States to be with me doing this time. She stayed with us for 6 months on this visit. It was great because I was diagnosed with Preeclampsia and was suppose to be on bed rest about a month or two prior to our daughter's arrival. There is no love like a mothers' love. She cooked and cleaned for us six months without hesitation. We enjoyed and loved every minute. We did not want her to do this type of service for us, but she insisted, and we didn't complain.

Mother was never in the way, she just wanted to go the church every Sunday. At that time, I was not ready to go to commit to church attendance like that yet. So I knew we lived across the street from the minister who we called 'Rev,' that was short for Reverend. His wife Elaine was precious and patient with me. I had strayed away from being committed to serving God as part of my life. Elaine and Rev. spent a lot of time with my mother in taking to her to church a lot. I was beginning to get jealous because mom laughed more with my minister neighbors than with me. This kept going for months to where they took her out to dinner prior to her departure and made their time with my Mom special. I felt like I was missing out on something: that special fellowship with church folks. My upbringing was coming back to me. *You know God's word says,* **"If you bring up a child in the way they should go, they shall not depart from it when they get old."** My mom did not complain about our lifestyle of not attending church, she just loved us through taking care of our new baby daughter and assisted us in balancing those duties out prior to her departure to Chattanooga. One day in the month of November, I had a taste for collard greens and corn bread, chitterlings, etc.—a real soul food meal. I cooked these special Southern foods and cleaned the house too on hands and knees in my ninth month of pregnancy. Just as I sat down to feast and became full, our baby girl was in a hurry to come out of the oven.

When I arrived at the hospital, I was almost at the delivery stage, but the Southern delicacies wanted to come out too. My stomach contents came up and went flying on the walls of the hospital while I was in labor. Leamon started to help the nurses clean the walls and I was shouting at telling him that I am the one in labor and needed all his undivided attention. He was ashamed what I did and felt obligated to help clean it up between my highs and lows of labor pains. About three hours later, our daughter Leamona was born.

It seemed like mother's instincts came natural the moment I saw our daughter. She was days old and started choking while lying on her back even though I laid her on her stomach. She turned purple from choking on milk and could not burp. I did not know CPR for Infants, but I sucked her noise, mouth and airway clear. I did not even think of what I was doing, mother's instincts kicked in to save my child. At five months old, Leamona was in a walker with a pillow propping her up; she would push on her legs early and started walking at nine months. Her doctors could not believe it. Leamona was an independent baby. She was tough and gentle. She grew up fast and wanted to do everything her way as much as she could.

Leamon and I waited to have kids after 7 years of marriage at my request. I wanted to ensure that Leamon Jr. would still be there to help raise her, and he had no intention to abandon his fatherly and husbandly duties. When Leamona came into our lives, I was a serious mother and very protective. We teamed up and did what we could do as a dual military couples in setting the best example as parents including being there and support her at every stage of growing up.

I knew a personal relationship with God was missing. I started attending the Chapel Nine service on North Fort Lewis and started to take God more seriously. The mothers of the Gospel Service prayed for me in a circle. I remember thinking that the praying was too long and attempt to easily exit the circle. They had formed a tight circle and I didn't want them to notice I was gone, but I couldn't get out of that circle without interrupting the praying process. By the way, they took the time to pray for me after I shared something personal with them. So, I began to listen to their words and close my eyes and shortly afterwards, I found myself weeping uncontrollably. My heart and mind was open for correction from the Holy Spirit, open to receive love and guidance from the chapel women who displayed a lot of love and patience with me. I came back to church over and over again. I wanted to do something and did not know which area to serve in, but, there was a kitchen that the women always served soldiers and their families in. It was great. I knew the kitchen was my comfort zone.

I began serving at every possible opportunity. I took our daughter with me everywhere I went with the women of the chapel. I couldn't stop serving people even to the point of exhaustion. I needed to learn how to be a woman of God and balance what He has for me to do with church folk, my family and taking care of me too. It came natural to me to serve anyone, almost anywhere. I learned that if I followed my heart in serving, everything would work out, in every area of my life. God's word taught me not to judge people because He is the Judge of all and everything. I had to totally trust in Him and not people. This came with growing in Christ through study, fellowship and practice what I was learning. I knew how my mother raised me; therefore, I came to the conclusion that I needed to be around other Christian mothers when I wasn't around my mother. Trial and error were the keys of being consistent in pursuing spiritual growth.

There was so much that could stir up unbelief with the wrong influences in my life. I saw that trying to keep up with a dual military status with children was even more of a test. Both of us wore the uniform, were in charge of soldiers and equipment in addition to having numerous other tasks. After a full day of soldiering, I still had to come home and be the wife, mother and everything to everybody. When I stayed connected to God's word and fellowship with women, who were trying to live right, take care of their families, be a good friend to their husbands and exemplify Christian attributes daily; through trial and error and praying I was sustained by God to do what is right. I was stable-minded in all I did for God and my family. I could hear Him saying, **"I will never leave you nor forsake you"**

Amazingly, God always sends people in our lives to assist us when we needed assistance. We needed childcare and didn't want to put her in a regular facility on base until she was older. I don't remember how we met this Spanish lady, but she needed the money and we needed her love and support. She needed to trust us to pay her the maximum that we could afford and we needed her to take care of our daughter when we went to work. There were times when we both went to the Field (Military War Training Exercises) at the same time. We were profoundly grateful for all the support God sent our way. I knew to trust in God for everything, because he had always made a way out of no way. He was the foundation on which we stayed married. Thanks be to God, we were able to stay together in all the various military assignments from the beginning to the end of my 21 year tenure. I went to military chapels to clock in church time with women from all walks of life then I was challenged to practice believing by acting on getting involved with the Women of the Chapel. Around 1989, we came down on orders to serve in the Republic of Korea in Seoul. Once again, we had to make huge decisions for our daughter because we had heard war stories about taking your kids to such a place. I knew I could trust no one other than my mother, Lillie Bell Rivers, so I called her and she open her heart to us. Without hesitation, she said that she was praying that God would open up doors for her to spend more time with her granddaughter. Wow! God sure did answered her prayers because Leamona was the eighteenth grandchild and Mom always wondered if she would be around to see me have grandchildren for her to enjoy too. Mother watched every move our daughter made. Although, my mother's love was priceless, we paid her well for her time and love while we were stationed overseas.

Our daughter was in God's Hands inside my Mother's hands. I came from a large family and I am the youngest of six. Mom kept Leamona close to her and my oldest sister mainly. When Leamona fell and had a bump on her head, Mother was so apologetic for this accident. Mother wanted our daughter's stay with her to be magic and magic it was in the Lord's Presence. You see, Mother set a Godly example with consistent love in her life. She served other senior ladies including my Granny. Leamona told me that she would have to take care of me when I get old because her Granny took care of her Great Granny who was mean to her. So, she would have to take care of me if I needed her to even though I was mean to her. During the War: Operation Desert Storm two years had gone by on this assignment. When we returned from Korea and went to pick up our daughter, she knew who we were, but she was afraid of us when we had on our military uniforms. It took a while for her to be comfortable with us again. We knew then that we would keep our family together on future assignments. Life seems tough when there are rules and structure at a young age. Leamona called me the fun sucker often, especially in her teenage years. Being dual military parents, our daughter did not have a lot of free time on her hands. Trying to balance between military and civilian life, we stood as a team in the next upcoming tour back to Korea.

Mental Stability

I have to think on the Word of God as I learn it because of the difference it makes in my every day decision making. *As a man think, so is he!* I am able to get out of life what I put into it from my thoughts. When my thoughts are in line with the Word of God; literally, "*I can do all things through Christ Jesus who strengthens me.*" I would distribute love in all required duties and tasks. I loved hard, in all I did, and I put my heart and energy into it with precision. From serving my family to serving God, while serving people He put in my path. Although, my exposures with people of all walks of life had been mainly with soldiers, church folk, military groups and many other families, I loved everyone. Sometimes, it was easy for people to take advantage of me because I needed to give to someone or just anyone, as a matter of fact. I strove on the need to serve and love because it completed me. I had to learn not to expect the same from people when I share my life, gifts and time with them. My life is a reality because of God the Father, Son and Holy Spirit's grace and mercy upon me. I could have been born during slavery and not have a voice to express the difference it makes having Christ in my life. I could have been dead and sleeping in my grave. I could have been in prison for decisions that were optional for me. My mental state is only as strong as my connection and relationship with the Word of God through the Holy Spirit's distributing to me understanding and wisdom, as I seek HIM. I am learning to *walk by faith and not by sight.* It is not about me or how I feel.

Emotions and feelings can be deceiving if you don't have a relationship with God and are not trained in His Word. *Life and death are in the power of the tongue*. In the 80s and 90s, I needed to believe for healing, I had to listen to Christian tapes and read books to build my faith. I have read several books by well know men and women of God and found out that I don't have to be perfect to tell my story. I can be who God has created me to be for starts and allow Him to mold me into the woman, He would so graciously allow me to become. I don't have to compare myself with people to learn that there will always be people more educated, more beautiful, more crafted and more well-known than me, no matter what level I am in life. I know that *that all things are possible to them that believe.* Therefore, I can go boldly to the throne of God in prayer and believe Him for myself to succeed at the level of my own Faith in all I do. I can rise above hurt and pain from people who have contributed to mental abuse and my distrustfulness by people who turned their backs on me when I needed them the most. I had to learn that being alone with temptation that was enticing me to do my fleshly will is a constant struggle, without God's word in my life. I had to learn by trial and error on testing God's Word for myself to overcome partiality. My mother inspired me to take parenting a level higher in acknowledging Christ as my Guide and Helper in raising my kids. He would be the One to more explicitly help me learn to communicate with them at their level of understanding. No matter what I am doing, my husband is consistent in providing for and loving our family, especially when life gets tough. My sister Gloria Jean taught me to be a sturdy woman and to be willing to do what you have to do for your family's environment and wellness regardless of who supports you or not. The Holy Spirit is here to be our Helper and our Comforter. He taught me to rely on Him for all I desire to do. He is the Guide as I tell the world how personal He is in my life. Trusting in God and not people is what made a difference when I went through trials and tribulations.

If you have a void in your life and you can't seem to make it or shake it off, try God. He and only He can fill the voids we have. For example, you can still be very lonely and have everything you desire in life. But you will never be lonely when you have a relationship with God, the Father, Son and Holy Spirit. Your days are longer because you have a burden on your shoulders to make your life the way you think it should be. You can lift the burden by living daily for Christ and having fun in His Presence and His Word.

Try God!!! He will amazingly fill your heart, lead and guide you to **peace that surpasses all understanding.**

Fruit Cake

"I eat the nuts out of the fruit cake,
because I don't like cooked, mushy fruit."

To me, fruitcake is a desert in which the good, the bad and the ugly are wrapped up all in one package. It's like life, sometimes you have to accept it all and pull out what you don't like and apply what you have learned from it all and use it to go forward. At the age of 13 years old, a man came to my sister's apartment to acknowledge to me that he was my father. This made life confusing for me.

I saw a man, who I will call John, sitting in the dining room in a chair against the wall. He called my name and asked me to sit on his lap. Now being the old soul that I was, my first response was, "why I need to sit on a strangers lap and who are you?" John said, "I am your father." I told him that you are crazy, my daddy is dead. He said, "Go in the living room and ask your mother." I asked my Mom, "Is this my dad?" My Mom had this look on her face of shyness and embarrassment. Then, my big sister Jean spoke up and said, "This is your real dad." Mom gave me a gesture to listen to what John had to say. You see there had been no man around me while I was growing up. I didn't listen to men much because I had a loving mother, a strong big sister, and a mighty feisty Granny. These women made me strong through their existence in my life. Aggressiveness and boldness came natural for me. I had no problem speaking up for myself.

I went back into the dining room to see what John had to say. He asks me again to sit on his lap. I did cautiously with the intent to harm him if he tried anything. We used to live on East 14th Street prior to moving inside the projects and I had to be a tough kid for protection when I wasn't around my mother. I carried myself in a confident way. Even when I did not understand words and definitions; I had wisdom from above, my Granny used to tell me. I looked at John hard as he tried to explain that he was my biological father. Then I became speechless for the first time in my life. All of a sudden, I regrouped in my thinking with several questions; not giving him a change to answer the previous question. I asked: "Why you come now and where have you been?" "Why haven't you helped my Mother with me?" "Don't you know we live in the projects on Welfare?" He said that his sister, (I will call her Ms. G.) keeps in touch with my Mother. He said that if he tried to answers my questions, I would not understand. Then he told me that his mother wanted to meet me because she knew I existed. He mentioned that she lived in Buffalo, New York. Now, this caught my attention because I wanted to travel anywhere new at anytime. If I could use him to do this, then so be it. He said that his niece and her husband would take me to see my other grandmother.

For some reason, somehow, I suppressed the reality of what just happened, because I wanted to travel out of the city safely with anybody. Then, I got excited, as young people do, and asked Mother if I could go meet him in Buffalo, New York. I knew nothing of this man John, but obviously, my big sister and Mother did. If they trusted him, then I would go and have fun, I thought. This is what was on my mind. I felt special for a moment. Wow! I am going to New York! That following summer came and my Aunt V. and her handsome husband picked me up in a light blue Cadillac. I had the whole back seat to myself. Mother had packed me my favorite, hotdogs, sodas, chips, etc. We ate a lot of processed meats back then. We left early at day break and arrived at night in New York. I had eaten all my food after several hours.

At the time, Aunt V. was nice to me, but I kept alert as much as possible. We arrived late in the evening. They dropped me off at an apartment with a young adult lady who had a toddler. We had the same name, and after I awoke the next morning, I realize instantly that I looked like this lady. We had the same features and smile. I had plenty of questions. She did not and could not explain much to me. I realized later that my visit was a secret in town. I went to meet my Dad's mother, my grandmother, and I noticed that she was ill and lived alone most of the time. I refused to stay there with her per my dad's request because in her basement, she had this enormous dog. It was a Rottweiler. I had never seen anything on four legs that huge before and fear set in. I was afraid he would get to me. John wanted me to stay with his mother overnight, I spoke up quickly. No way! I can't stay here. She doesn't seem as if she would be able to protect me from that dog in the basement. John became angry with me because

I spoke up about where I wanted to stay in front of his mother. We left her home and he took me back to the lady named Deborah's apartment.

At this point, I wanted answers from this lady. She only told me that John was her father too and I was to stay put with her until Aunt V. came to take me back home. It turned out, my visit was for his mother who was terminally ill and she wanted to see her granddaughter before she left this world. This was the only reason I was there in New York. John did not spend time with me at all. I wasn't surprise because after all, he was unreliable from the beginning. I had the nerve to get angry. When my half-sister wasn't looking, I went for a walk. I needed to think about what was happening to me. Why did I have these emotions of not feeling special like John made me feel when he invited me to come to New York? I only came because I thought this man was indeed my father, as confirmed by my mother, who agreed for me to depart from her and go with him. I came for an adventure anyway to get away from the projects. And an adventure I got.

During my walk, I walked far. I just wanted to get out and see whatever I could prior to Aunt V's arrival. I had walk so far, I ended up in some projects somewhere in Buffalo. It was hot and I became weak and thirsty. At this point, I needed help. I had no ID on me to prove who I was. I didn't know John's phone number to call him, nor did I know my half sister's phone number. I was looking for someone to come to my aid. Somehow, I was looking at apartment doors to see who door was open for me to ask for some water. Amazingly, I saw this lady, through her screen and knock on her door. I said, "Maim, I need some water." She said to me, "I can tell you are not from here because you talk different." She ask me, "where are you from and why are you walking alone in a place like this?" This lady was about my mother's age and immediately, I felt safe. I told her my story about how I got to New York and why. I was filled with emotions and teared up. I needed someone to talk to who would not judge me. She gave me some water and donuts. I felt love from her, but I knew it was getting late in the afternoon. About an hour later, we heard people calling my name. I came to the door and saw John. I was relieved because I couldn't give any information about him or his family other than his name. She seemed to know of him, but would not go into details with me. He gave the lady a huge hug and gave her money. Then he raised his voice telling me he was about to call the police to help find me. He said, "I told your mother that you would be safe and I could not go back to Chattanooga if something had happened to you. Are you Crazy?!" He yelled at me saying that I missed the tour to Niagara Falls. Aunt V and husband left without me on the tour. As I put my head down walking toward his car, he asks me how I got this far in the heat. I had no answers. I was ready to go home. I was very disappointed that things did not turn out better than I expected. I had no control over John's dissatisfaction with me. I never went back to his mother's house. My half sister told me that John had a secret life and she could not tell me much. I later learned that John was married during the time I was conceived. At that moment, his wife did not know I was in town. I began to see that this half-sister cared a little for me, but she explained that John did not think she was good enough to be his daughter because she had a baby by a Spanish guy. Her baby girl was a beautiful little girl. I said, "That's nothing, I know several young girls where I'm from with no baby daddies at all and at least you have a man". Okay, I was getting back to my old soul self again. Here I was again, talking like I was an old lady. This sister said that she enjoyed my visit and she explained to me that she had heard stories about me. The next day, I was on my way back to Chattanooga.

It seems that the ride back was faster and no one talked to me much. They dropped me off back home to my Mother and left quickly. I shared the story with my big sister and Mother about my experience and trip. I felt numb for a while. I discussed my journey in a funny and entertaining way to my family, but deep down I was hurting. My conclusion was men weren't honest and reliable. I had matured leaps and bounds overnight. I thought that the reason I had no man around was because my father was dead. And now, knowing that I had one alive and doing well was puzzling to me still. Back in the day, people did not talk about who got pregnant by whom. They kept everything a secret. This seemed normal for them, but I never understood it. Now-a-days, people talk about everything using technology where information and gossip travels faster than the speed of sound.

John called my Mother after I got back home, but the communications faded away for years. When John made contact with me through my Mother, he was around 72 years old and he too drove a new light blue beautiful Cadillac. I was about 29 years old when I saw him again. By this time, I had been in the military for about 12 years. We talked on the phone briefly, maybe once or twice. I came home on leave from the Army and John saw me briefly. This is the time he felt he needed to talk to me personally as an adult. I told him that I had a hard time trusting my husband to be there for me because all I ever saw was men neglecting their responsibilities. I had our daughter Leamona with me at the time I met with him in Chattanooga. We talked for a while in this new car while sitting outside of the Buy-Low Grocery Store on 23rd Street. I remembered Leamona jumping over his car seats and he raised his voice at her. At this point, I was able to raise my voice at him telling him not to talk to her like that because this was my child. And when I had her, I knew that I could take care of her if her father ever left me like he did. I further explained that I could afford the expenses as an Army Soldier, so don't go there. I did not play around when it came to my child. All the Army training would surface in the peak of the moment. John's life was always a mystery to me. We saw each other maybe once more later that week. We took a picture together at K-Mart, because I wanted proof that he existed. I had put on my Army records that my dad was decease because I did not know anything about John to claim him to be my father. He did not raise me. I honestly don't know if he ever saw me before I was 13 years old. I never felt good about him, nor for that matter any man. I was hard on all men because they had the potential to harm me with distrust. We talked more and more on the phone when I was stationed in Korea. His wife, Ms. Doris, I will call her, knew of me and wanted to meet me. I was excited about that and we talked over the phone often while I was stationed in Korea. Before I could meet her, she had a fall in their bathroom and experienced an Aneurism and died. John was so hurt and depressed for this tremendous and great lost of his wife. I sent him money in a card and we continued to talk with the intention of seeing one another again soon. I always had mixed emotions about my dad situation. I just trusted God no matter what because I had no control over how things had turned out. I was praying on a Friday night around 9:00 p.m. upstairs in our family home and John came to my mind and heart. At that moment, I spoke to him while I was praying saying the following: "What you failed to do for me is between you and God. I thank God that I had a chance to experience knowing you existed. I am grateful that you had the chance to meet with me and get to know me as a woman. I release you from the burden of your failures concerning me, because God has always kept me when I didn't realize it." I remembered this as if it were yesterday. I spoke from my heart. I let God know that my thoughts and heart were filled with gratitude because where I am in life means everything to me because of His Presence.

The following Monday morning, I received a phone call from my Aunt V telling me that John had been shot and killed. He was pronounced dead at midnight on Friday. This was within the same timeframe on the West Coast when the Holy Spirit led me to pray and pour my heart out to God for just being there for me during all of my young years of adventures, life's challenges and heartbreaks. I felt numb and without emotions. Yet, I felt satisfied that God gave me closure in Washington State. It was amazing that during a tragic event, which took place in Buffalo, New York, over four thousand miles away, at the same time that my dad was going through this horrific experience, I was offering up forgiveness for his years of neglect. My Aunt V told me not to call or contact anyone in Buffalo, New York about what happened to John because it was not safe for me and my family. I didn't ask questions because I knew John lived a secret and double life that I wasn't involved in. It was a life that I didn't understand. But, God had never failed me, when I most needed Him to come through. When experiences were unexplainable, I cherished His Presence each time. Here He was again, on the scene to bring closure with my dad.

I believe that there are no illegitimate kids born in this world. Every child is born with the love of God. He loved us so much that He gave His only begotten Son to die on the cross for us, so we may have life and life more abundantly. God's word is comfort when I allow it to minister to my heart and to heal my wounds of distrust.

Decision Making

Although Howard School had first through twelfth grade, the middle school kids were segregated to a white school across town—East Side Junior High. There were white kids everywhere. I did not feel like I was a part of their world, therefore, I created my own world. Alone with receiving basic education, I had a choice to learn how to do upholstery, cooking or sewing. The skill of sewing helps me tailor all my cloths that do not fit my body shape. Although I did not tolerate being mistreated in any form, I was not a trouble maker. I don't remember exactly, but something happened in the class room and I was not afraid of the teacher or students. I ended up in the principal's office. He was a black man. I had not seen a black man in authority before outside of church. At least, I never paid attention to it, until that moment. I will call him Mr. Bookings. He picked up a huge paddle (stick) and told me he needed to give me three licks. I looked at him and explained to him the following, "Sir, if you hit me, I will take that paddle and throw it out the glass window! I can't let you hit me; no man will hit me and get away with it!" Mr. Bookings called my mother to tell her that if I don't take the paddle, I will be expelled from school. He would not have called my Mother if I had not resisted his paddling. My Mother quickly explained to him that he could not spank me. Mr. Bookings expelled at me and my Mother took a taxi cab to my school across town to pick me up and take me home. I told Mother that no man could hit me. Mother was very composed, which is so unlike me at times. She just looked at me and said she loved me, not matter what. I enjoyed a couple of days home with my Mother. Although, I don't recall what happened, I never experienced problems in school again. I had a reputation by the time I got back to school. The funny thing is, I didn't know what the reputation was. I felt like I had accomplished something that I was not quite aware of, but it gave me a sense of well-being that I couldn't explain.

I was always a confident and strong young girl. My Granny always would say that I was an old soul. Also during junior high while I was 14 years old, I lied on a job application about being 15 years old, so I could work my first job at a newly built Wendy's Restaurant on Broad Street. I felt it was necessary because I needed to help my mother take care of me. I wasn't the kind of child who needed to shop a lot, but I did like nice things. I had a birthday by the time the manager found out my correct age. I had learned the ropes by then and I was too good for him to fire me. At least that is what I like to think. I worked there off and on throughout high-school and also at the Woolworth's Department Store downtown. I did whatever I could to stay comfortable while I was in school.

When I had a change to return to my old neighborhood for High School, I chose to attend school further out. I lied about my address so I could attend Brainerd High School. In the last 10 years, I went to see my second grade teacher, the late Emma Reed, and little did I know she was on the District School Board. They knew I was out of district, and Ms. Reed said she told them to leave me alone because I wasn't hurting anything if I traveled cross district lines. She explained that I had perfect attendance, kept my grades up and never caused any trouble. I thought I was doing something clever and getting away with it. God had someone planted in a position of authority, so I could get grace and favor to attend the school of my choice. Sometimes in life we think we are getting over by doing wrong or being sneaky about something; but I know that **everything done in the darkness shall come to light.** I always had my Mother's support in whatever I wanted to do because it seemed that I was always trying to leave the area that I was living in to better myself. Although it was not dangerous or threatening in any way, there were a few bullies that I did not want to go to High School with because they kept up too much drama. I wanted to start anew as often as possible, every chance I got. Besides it was in my blood to stay on the move.

Well, I arrived at my new school and got to know a few students. Ironically, I met Mr. Booking's daughter, and I ask her if her dad ever spanked them with a paddle. She said, "No." So I told her to tell him that she goes to school with me. When I saw her the next day, I ask her did she tell her dad and she said, "Yes." Then I asked, "What did he say?" She said, "He didn't say anything and he said he couldn't remember you." I knew that she was lying because she kept her distance from me throughout remainder of our high school years. I was careful not to start any trouble at school because I knew I was out of zone and the district would send me back to my neighborhood school. I did not want the students to know where I was from because I needed to keep a low profile. Some students who rode the city bus knew that I was on the bus before and after they got on or off. I tried to reside at my Granny's sister, Aunt Carrie's house, but I wasn't good enough for her, I thought. And when I became an adult, I confronted her and she did not remember rejecting me. Becoming a middle age Woman of God, I realize that you don't want people in your house as you get older. I tried so hard to live in the community where I went to school that I ask Mother if I could stay with my former-sister in-law. I stayed with her for about a year or two until things got hot with her and my oldest brother again. She had married my brother's best man from their wedding. Later she and my brother remarried. Praise God, they are still married today. Although things change as the years go by, this sister in-law is well loved by me. Then, I had to catch the bus the remainder of my high school tenure.

I had perfect attendance because I didn't want to bring any attention to myself. I knew that I could come to school when I was sick, which was rare, and leave after a certain time and would not be marked absent. I dated during high school and my boy-friend's whole family was nice to me. Mrs. Williams was icing on the cake. She took me to Dr. Boas on Market Street and told him I was her niece from out of town and he gave me some Lo-Oval Birth control pills without question. I hid this from mother until after she signed the papers for the military. My mom gave me no response, because I assured her that because of that, I did not have babies and now I could go freely into the world. Mrs. Williams was protecting her son and me, and I am still grateful for this today because I was able to plan becoming a parent when I was ready. Having sex outside of marriage isn't God plan for a man and women. His word tells us to marry first. In my experience, I don't remember my church leaders breaking this area of life to me the way leaders do now. Maybe I was just a teenager not paying attention because I was too busy doing my own thing.

Sometimes, I would spend the night at my boy friend's house. I would have to sleep with his sister. She was the only girl. The family treated me like family, but sometimes she didn't want me around because I was invading her space. Sometimes, I teased her a lot; but since I wanted to keep the peace so that I could come back over their house, I did things to help her mother. Although I was a teen, I ran her kitchen when I fried fish and made home-made slaw. They loved it! My oldest sister Gloria

Jean was a cook, so I just imitated her in controlling the kitchen when I cooked. From cleaning to cooking, I am quick with my hands. I enjoyed my first love tremendously. He gave me my first two "promise rings," which represented a marriage commitment. When I joined the Army, I gave him the opportunity to move to Fayetteville, North Carolina to start a life together. This was before I mentioned to Leamon that shacking wasn't good enough for me. We were different: he didn't want to leave home and I made my home wherever I was living. This made it easy to grow closer to my best friend. I even had those two to meet when we came to Chattanooga to visit. I wanted to observe them side by side because I loved both men. Although I was still in love with my high school sweetheart for years, the military way of life had already started making its mark on my thinking. My best friend was my soon to be husband.

I had a special friend name Reggie and two other close friendships in high school. I admired Reggie because he was filled with unexplainable wisdom and we cliqued very well. The problem was, he had a girl friend and I had a boyfriend. My boyfriend was a popular dude because he played sports and maintain high academics on the other side of town. I didn't open up to too many people because I wanted to keep a low profile because I was from the projects on the Southside. I wanted to keep it a secret as much as possible so I could stay in school in this particular district.

My classmates joked about me having perfect attendance from sixth through twelfth grade at our graduation. Everyone laughed, but I didn't care. I laughed too, because I had finished my tenure at the school of my choice and I had secretly joined the Army at 17 years old, six months prior. Thinking I was out of there once again. No one knew except my Mother and big sister and a select group of people. I did not even tell my high school sweetheart and his family because his mother had purchased a second first promise ring after I had lost the first one. She wanted me to be her daughter in-law and at that time, I wanted to be her daughter in law too. I love them deeply for being there for me to this day. I did whatever it took to stay out in the community where my school was in, so people could see that I had connections with the area sometimes. The reality is, I was ashamed of the projects, but soon grew out of it my senior year. I was called an Oreo often for attending a mixed colored school. I remember after a football game, we defeated Howard High, I walked proudly back to our apartment with people who knew I went to Brainerd High School and didn't care. After graduation, I worked at Woolworth's, and applied for a job at Tennessee Valley Authority (TVA). I received a letter after I was on active duty to come for an interview. They told me that if I chose to get out at the end of my enlistment, I could come back and still make that interview for employment. The Army became my employer for life because sometimes my tenure seems to last forever, but I have no regrets. I had my best friend by my side and the World's Greatest Mother's prayers.

A Mother's Love

Mother set the best example of a Godly woman for our family. I can honestly take to my grave my experience with her to be exactly what I needed. She lived for God and her family. I never heard mother talk about people in the negative way that so many women do now-a-days. I experienced a lot of parents talking down to their children. I often heard one of my friend's mother called her daughter a monkey and say that she was ugly. And to this day, that same girl calls her daughter names and mistreats her because that is all she experienced with her mother. Lillie Bell, my mother, was meek and humble and never raised her voice at me in a way to demean or discredit me as a young girl growing up trying to find out who I was and what I would become. My Mom's doors and ears were always open to her kids and grandkids, no matter what was happening in her own personal life. If we had drug problems or health problems, mom's place was the place to come for rest and restoration. It was a place to back up and regroup when mistakes were made that resulted in financial hardships too.

A mid-size truck that is going 60 miles per hour requires about 600 feet to come to a complete stop. Therefore, if it had a sudden impact, it would be a tragic scene with no possible opportunity to be restored to working condition. At best, it would probably end in the junkyard and used as scraps. It would only be good for other people to come and get parts from it to fix other trucks of its kind. There were times in our lives when we were like a truck traveling at 60 miles per hour and coming in contact with a wall. Sometimes my mother looked at the tragic scene of our lives and did her best to pick us up and salvage what she could while believing God to handle the rest. She would nurture and serve us back to a healthy state of mind from circumstances to go back out in the world and try again.

Before my sister, Lizzie passed away from Lupus, she had to move back home. Mom was always ready to accept any of her children with open arms of love at anytime, day or night. Mom rented a larger apartment to accommodate my sister and her family for a while. One time, I came home on leave and my teenage niece had a temper tantrum and threw the dinner that was on the gas stove top to the floor out of anger. I attempted to whip her, but she hit me back. This opened doors for a different level of physical altercation. My mother was hurt, but my sister seemed thrilled because she could not do anything thing with her daughter's disrespect due to her illness. I became afraid of possible domestic violence charges. If the police had been notified, I was going to get into trouble with the Law, because I was a soldier home on leave visiting my family and had this incident. My niece chose to go across Market Street in the high rise apartments for seniors to stay with my grandmother until I departed. I could not tolerate a child disrespecting my mother after she had cooked a meal for her family. We were all hungry and ready to eat. Therefore, I had to go out and purchase pizza because they did not do delivery in the project neighborhood. Our daughter saw this incident and suppressed this experience for years until she was turning 13 years old. The things parents do has an impact on our kids. When our daughter Leamona became a teen, she started to express sadness. I never knew she remembered this incident. I had to call my niece for Leamona to talk to her. Then she explained to her that she was not angry at me about what happened and she still loves her aunt. Leamona needed this confirmation from my niece because when she was younger, experiencing this commotion affected her state of mind of what happens to teenagers. I hugged her and told her I love her and will set the best example possible, as a mother, with God's help and respect is crucial in a home amongst everyone.

I loved my Mom because she would just listen to my problems and the crazy things I used to do and she never responded to me in judgment. Behind the scenes, I know she was a praying woman. I saw this with my own eyes. I only remembered one whipping. When I didn't get along with one particular sister in-law, mother would be hurt, but she never took sides. She would always say, "You know better." And I did, but when anger set in, knowing and doing went out the window. I wasn't able to overlook hurt and pain from intentional gossiping and meddling. When people thought they were better than us, Mom set the example for me by not responding. Me, on the other hand, I wanted to show people that I didn't care. Our mother was content and material possessions did not drive her. Raising a family in the church was her priority. Mom respected God and everyone around her whether they showed love or concern for her or not.

Missionary Baptist Church was my first church and its operations were run mostly by relatives on my mother's side, which consisted of aunts, uncles and cousins. I wanted to get away from some of our family seniors, so I joined Olivet Baptist Church around the corner. I caught my mom's church bus and walked around the corner a few months, and came back in time to catch my mom's church bus back home. Then, I realized I needed to give my life to Christ, so I accepted Jesus Christ as my Lord and Savior and Pastor Robert Richards baptized me. Then I joined the Usher-Board. After finding out about my dad, I needed Jesus more than ever. Then I was able to catch my own church bus that came around to pick up people for church who did not have a car. I was an usher and served proudly until I went to high school. I didn't go to church much during that time. I was trying to find myself on the other side of town and transportation was limited. I had matured leaps and bound as a young lady. I seemed to foresee the negative impact in advance if I made poor decisions by allowing the wrong kind of people access to my personal space. I always kept thinking how God had me and I acted like I was in the palm of His hands. Therefore, I had to do my part and trust Him to keep me safe from harm as I moved around the city on buses. Mother was a praying woman and the peace she displayed in her motherly atmosphere surely surpassed my understanding. You know, this is the peace that comes only from God.

THE WORLDS GREATEST MOTHER

Lillie Bell Rivers was a woman of peace and woman of God whose atmosphere was loved by everyone who came in contact with her. She was content with where she was and who she was. She did not display a desire to fit into a particular group of women other than at church, because she was plugged into God's Word. I observed her praying a lot, fellowshipping with one or two Christian's women regularly. She displayed love and respect for her family.

Wants Verses Needs!

My daughter and I went to the Annual Puyallup Fair. One year, instead of me going and having a great time with Leamona, I was distracted by the Campers and Recreational Vehicles (RVs) on display as we entered the fair grounds. I chose to go to check them out. I felt that the Lord wanted me to have the desires of my heart. Therefore, I started looking and looking, and suddenly a crafty salesman approached me to shop. Wow! This was great! My Chevy, G20 Van wasn't enough for me anymore. It was just paid off anyway. It was nice and roomy with a fold out bed in the rear with an extended cab. When the Van ever needed repair, my husband is an excellent mechanic. So replacing our Van wasn't a mutual option. But, I thought since he was on a military field training exercise, I could test drive one for a short while. He knew that it was always my dream to own an RV. You know sometimes, we see something we want and don't need. I prayed to God that if He would open doors for me to get an RV, I would be so grateful. Now, sometimes we get in our own way and open up doors for ourselves. When God opens up doors, they are doors that no man can close, if we are obedient and humble in listening to His directions for our lives.

I had no idea that I would drive home in a brand new RV Camper. Later that night, the thought of the terrible consequences, stress and possible disaster in my life came to my mind. The brilliant salesman made a deal I could not refuse. Leamona said, "Mother, you are going to get in trouble with Dad." Of course, I was grown and I ignored my young daughter's warning. When the contract was drown up, I failed to read it, so I glanced at it and signed it because he said that I needed my husband's signature to make the sale final. The salesman helped clean out my van and loaded my stuff inside my new Camper. It was green and white with a microwave, bed, cabinets and no bathroom. Although I thought I was doing something great, I was blind as a bat. I drove off the lot at the Fair cautiously. The smell of newness filled my lungs like perfume with great satisfaction. I cranked up the music while driving it home. I couldn't believe that I did it, so I had to show somebody quick. I went by a friend's house and honked my horn like a wild woman. She came out and saw how beautiful my camper was and looked inside. Then she asks me where my husband was. I thought for a moment that what he doesn't know won't hurt. Besides, I was taking it back if he didn't sign the contract.

I drove home and came up the drive way and entered the house through the front door. Therefore, I did not see my husband's car in the garage. When I came in the house, I saw some military boots against the wall neatly placed in the living room and I wondered for a moment; who could be in my house because those boots were not there when we left the house earlier. I called my husband's name and he answered, "Woman where you been this time of night?" Leamona ran down the hallway to Dad. At that moment, I was shaking some keys saying, "Honey, I have a surprise for you." As always, he responded, "what have you done? I said, "Come see. It's beautiful." He wouldn't come out of the bedroom at all. He hollered down the hallway saying," How much does it cost?" I said, "I don't know!" So I got the papers and hollered down the hallway; "$67,000 with a 10% interest rate!" We were new home owners, and the RV Camper cost almost more than our home at the time. I heard my husband say, "You go get my van back or don't you come back!" He put Leamona to bed and told me to go. It was around 11:30p.m. When I departed to go back to the Fairground looking for that salesman, I was driving back thinking how excited it was to drive a new RV Camper anyway. I finally arrived and they were on their last customer. The salesman looks at me astonished. I entered his office nonchalantly. I explained to him that my husband was home from the field (over night military training in the woods) and I needed to give back his RV Camper and get my van. He said, "No can do, because I have a buyer for your van and they will be by tomorrow morning to talk about a sales price." I told him that I would have to go home with him because I had nowhere else to go. I asked him to call his wife because I was coming home with him. He saw I was serious and explained to me that I had signed a contract. I reminded him that he told me that the contact wasn't final unless my husband signed it to make the sale official due to my credit.

At this point, I said, "Sir, I am sorry that I have to go home with you". He explained to me that I must be crazy to think I could go home with him. I was sincere because my husband meant business. The staff people who were ready to lock up laughed at him and told him to do the right thing. He had me sign some papers to void the sale and helped me put my stuff back in my van. While I was driving back home, I thought to myself how good God was to get me out of the mess I got myself into. My original purpose that day was to take our daughter to the Fair and have fun; instead, I took her on a mental roller-coaster. I finally got home around 1:30 a.m. I was exhausted. My husband, Leamon never brought up the situation to me again. I laughed about it when I told the story of what happened. But, God spared my family from financial ruin from my poor decision making.

You know, God knows what we need. **He will never leave us nor forsake us.** Even when we go off and do things on our own, God's grace and favor will sustain us. Sometimes we have to live with the consequences of not seeking His guidance through His Word. There are times we know right from wrong, but our desires can overturn what is reasonably right when we don't plug into a relationship with Him. How! Through studying His Word and fellowshipping with like minded people who believe that God is who He say He is. There are times we fall, but with the help of the Holy Spirit, we can get back up. **Knowing that everyone sins and falls short of the Glory of God** is nourishing to me because I don't have to feel bad about myself when I screw up. I have to repent by asking God to forgive me; then sometimes I have to go back and apologize to someone for something I did or said. In most cases, I still have to suffer the consequences for my actions and decisions. This is not always easy, **but with Christ, I can do all things through Him who strengthens me.**

People don't understand one another at times mostly because they don't see what is going on inside our hearts and minds. So judging one another is easy when you are on the outside looking in. I find that when I judge people, I am judged in the same way, and it doesn't feel good. Amazingly, Leamon never threw that RV Camper situation in my face; not even when we have disagreements. He is low key and very little seems to bother him. How many of us bring incidents from the past to support present unpleasant arguments? It's like throwing fuel on the fire. I am guilty of doing it sometimes. God has a way of convicting my spirit to make correction and adjustments through studying and listening to His preached word. Participating in worship and praise is a way that my heart is open to the Holy Spirit's voice speaking to me to change and be humble.

Farewell

My precious Mother, Lillie Bell Rivers, who went to be with the Lord, had an amazing impact on my life and she will live forever in my heart. From her, I learned how to love hard, serve with gratitude and stay away from 'people who don't mean yah any good.' Wow! What a Virtuous Woman, she was. I absolutely never saw her argue with neighbors and any other woman not even her own children. A quiet and timid women, unlike me, shined lighter that a candle in darkness. Her cheeks were dark and round, her skin was black and beautiful. When I was serving my second tour of duty in the Republic Seoul Korea, I kept in touch with Mother as often as possible. I noticed that she did not remember all the birthdays like she used to do, because everyone would receive a birthday card. This was a wakeup call for me that something was wrong. I used to get a box of pecans nuts in the mail annually for as long as I could remember during the holidays, and that stopped. Our conversations started to change from being long to just a few minutes here and there. I called my sister to see why Mother was changing. She said that Mom had a lot of pain in her side. I began to worry because I wasn't close to her to take over tending to her every need or care and just being there for her because she had always been there for everyone.

I came home on a leave of absence from the Army one time and found out Mom even had insurance on all her grown children and was attempting to put her grandkids on life insurance too. I encouraged her to stop and allow her adult children to take the responsibility for their own family's life insurance policies. I left home at 17 to join the Army, but while growing up, I never understood why Mr. Walton would come to the house for money often and write a note on a file for deposit. Mother never got a receipt for deposit down through the years. By the time I understood what was going on, I had been away, back and forward a few times. So Mom did cut down on the married sibling's life insurance and later, the remainder of adults. They eventually ended up on their own for life insurance as it should have been, in my mind anyway. Mother's illness progressed over the months. One day, I called Mom and she said to me clearly, "thank you for loving me, thank you for doing all you do for me down through the years and I love you very much". I had no idea that she was somehow saying good bye to me. I called my sister later that day to tell her of the comments Mom made. Weeks later, I got a Red Cross Message through the military to contact my family. I called my sister Jean who later explained to me that I needed to come home because Mom was asking about me and I needed to come home. Jean said the following, "Now when you see Mom, she is not the same. She has changed! The doctors say that she will not make it through. (This is hard to express!). I had no intention of believing what was told to me because I knew that I served a mighty God, **and nothing was impossible for Him to those that believed.** I came home on leave to see about Mother. I never thought for a moment that it would be my last time seeing her alive.

My husband, Leamon Jr., son, Leamon III and daughter, Leamona arrived in town late that night around 9:30p.m. It was too late to go the hospital. I sat on the floor in my sister's dining room alone, and came face to face with God's Presence. I asked Him, "Lord are you calling Mom home? Or do I need to fight a good fight of faith that she can pull through, while I know that You got her back? Lord is you calling her home?" I asked God and the Holy Spirit spoke to my heart loud and clear, "I am calling her home!" I felt my stomach drop. I was thinking Lord, what I'm I to do? How do I handle this? Then I received the following directions from the Holy Spirit. "When you see her, tell her that I will say to her, "Well Done My Good and Faithful Servant! Tell her that you will be alright and I will take care of you." At this moment, I felt that I was on a mission. The next morning around 7:00a.m., I awoke. Jean and I were at the hospital around 9:00a.m. Jean said, "Now remember, when you see Mom, she looks different." I was focused on the mission to tell Mom what the Holy Spirit said for me to tell her. When I got to her room at the hospital, I saw her body lying on a table with a thin sheet covering her with no pillow under her head. She was fragile. My emotions started to knick in heavy. I said out loud . . . "Emotions! Back Up! In Jesus' Name!"

I walked over to Mother, who had not spoken in days or weeks. I opened my mouth to speak to tell her what the Lord instructed me. Opening her yellow eyes filled with jaundice, in a loud voice, Mother blessed me with her voice saying, "Oh Yeah!" After that, I went on to complete God's message to her that He will welcome her to the Pearly Gates of Heaven with His arms open wide. Mom! God told me to tell you that He will take good care of me. Then, I asked Mom, can you see the light Mom! It's okay. I will be fine. You can let go! My mother hands were gripping my hand tighter. Then, all of a sudden, she let me go and never gave another response. It was as if she had received the closure that she needed to exit this world. God allowed her to experience this with her baby girl. The room became cool and breezy as I departed my mother's presence. In my heart, I felt God Himself was smiling while the Angels in Heaven were rejoicing.

Still on a mission! I walked toward the door where my sister was standing in awe and I told her let's make funeral arrangements and do what we have to do. I said, "That's Mother's shell in there Jean, but Mom is already gone. I showed no emotions. I didn't know how to at this point. Jean said, "I have never seen anything like this before!" I became a stronger woman of God instantly. The strength I displayed was not of me personally in the physical, but all Spiritual through Jesus Christ, my Lord and Savior. You know Jesus left us a Comforter. I said immediately after this experience, "Let's make Funeral arrangements. We went back to my sister house and began calling all the phone numbers in our Mother's phone book. We let them know that Mom was at the hospital and will not make it. Mom was moved to a room until death was pronounced on her by a doctor. Her body went through moans and groans of pain. I went and asked the hospital staff to give her something for pain. A white male nurse came out gladly to give Mother morphine. As he walked proudly down the hall, I saw him flicker the needle with his middle finger as if he was having fun. I could not respond because I was in the Mission Mode to get comfort to the body during this transition from life to death.

Later, several family members came in and out and during this time, I stayed mainly in the hallway looking in my Mother's room while waiting on her official death to be announced. My in-laws came to visit with my brothers and they were in there having more laughing moments about everything under the sun. I observed from a distance. Still in a Mission Mode or state of mind with a hard heart knowing that some relatives could have displayed more love to Mother with more respect while she was still able to receive it. This gathering was not enthusing to me! Now, I needed to take care of Mother's body and head back to the Army life with my husband. Then I left the hospital again, and this time when we were called back up to the hospital and I saw relatives on the outside and throughout the hallways crying about huge, deep down to the bones, the loss of our Mother, and others Grandmother. At the time, I still displayed no emotions because I was on a Mission. It was like an out of body experience.

Around 5pm, mother had officially passed away. So, I, along with Jean, waited for the Funeral Home to retrieve our Mother's body and no one else stayed. The side show and joking and laughing were gone and maybe I had an attitude and suppressed anger or emotions as we as humans sometime do. I just did not see anything be happy about. I observed the Mortuary personnel put my Mother's body in a bag and roll her out of the hospital building and into a van. Then the work started. Numbness was me for the next week. Knowing that Mother would be buried in a Veteran Cemetery on top of her late husband, Tressie T. Rivers, Sr. was comforting. We did not have to make the decision to where her body would be resting. The funeral was quiet. Many came to express their sympathy for our loss. Some relatives came out the woodwork to participate in the service. Again, I was still numbed, without emotions. It was important to me that the casket be closed. Upon arriving, I immediately had the Funeral Home people close the casket prior to the family arriving at the church. It was too much for me to see Mother lying there! After the funeral, we went to the closure. Leaving the National Veteran Cemetery for Soldiers, I felt comforted again knowing that her grave site would be kept up. I have visited her grave site on other occasions. But in my heart, I know that God has Mother and her shell no longer matters to me. With a sigh of relief, I was ready to head back to Seoul Korea to continue my tour of service and retire from the military.

I went on as usual, grieving in my own way. A female soldier asks me in the elevator after work one day if I was alright. I said yes and left it at that. She said that, "I don't know what I would do if my mom died." I told her that you will keep on living, that's what you will do! She went further to say that she never sees me crying or upset. I told her I do cry. I just do it alone on my own time and in my own space. Nonetheless, I continued to go through the motions of being in charge of Air Force Airmen, Navy Seaman and Army Soldiers: to include Korean civilians and other staff operations and maintaining equipment at the Demilitarize Military Zone (DMZ) while finishing up my active duty service in the United States Army,

United Nations Command. The pain was getting deeper and deeper. The closer I got to retirement, knowing that I had to return to the United States again and knowing that I did not have a mother—it gripped my heart with anguish.

Our youngest son, Leamon III, was only 9 months old when Mother passed. She only got to see his picture. She never held him in her arms. Gradually, I went through emotional changes both mentally and physically. About six months later, anger set in and I was mad at the world, but not God. Somehow, I knew that this area was untouchable and off limits to judge. I just talked to Him while letting Him know how much I missed her and needed more strength to endure the loss. You see, no one could take care of Mother like me. I was, I thought, the best child who gave her the most money and material things. Mom never made a difference in us period! Although, some siblings did not show Mother as much love, honor and respect, as I thought she deserved, she loved all of us equally and openly. Never have I heard negative comments from her about any of my siblings. I was the last at home with her and saw the love, meekness and contentment that was unexplainable. I just knew she was happy seeing her big family getting along and fellowshipping often. We never had fights and out of control arguments in our family. We were a loving family with as many flaws in life as other human beings. But the love that Mother rendered to us made her the most Christianized World's Greatest Mother to me.

Mother never cursed at us nor did she ever talk down to us. Although, it seemed easy to mistreat or abuse her because of how she carried herself so humbly and it never crossed my mind nor did I see anyone else do it. Mother loved and respected the mothers of her church and served everyone in her presence. Wow! What an example she set for me. And now, I see a lot of her qualities in me. I too love and serve the mothers in my church. I am still praying to be the humble and loving mother she was to me by being devoted to my family as well. She was my best friend, who I loved dearly.

Only God Can Truly Fill Voids in Life

If you feel lost and lonely, God can fill your void like nothing on earth. What am I talking about?

The down to the bone agony and frustrations that come from missing loved ones and those deep wounds in our hearts from hurts and pains generated as a result of other people's actions and conversations cannot be explained in words. However, a **cheerful heart is medicine and a broken spirit makes one sick**. When our heart is hard and closed from displaying love freely, we nurture negative vibes that can make us ill. Sometimes we cannot spring back on our power and we need God to personally come on the scene. He uses people, events, circumstances, and more to assure us that **He cares about everything that concerns us**.

I remember when my mother was alive, and I come home from the Army to visit, she would have family at the airport waiting on my plane to land to welcome me. This happened for the 19 years of my military career. After she went home to be with our Lord and Savior Jesus Christ, my first time coming home after her death, no one was waiting for me. In fact, the ride that came for me was late. I had to wait. I had never experienced not having greeters when I arrived home standing there with my mother. It was strange. I felt cold on a steaming hot sunny day and my spirit was damp. This was my first time coming back to the United States after retiring from the military in Korea. I was hurt and wanted to cry, but I didn't want my kids to notice the real reason for my tears. I thought this was a wakeup call that people only did nice gestures for me for our mother's sake. It wasn't from their hearts to show me love. I only came home every 3 to 5 years. One thing I know for sure is that my sister, Jean kept cooking trying to keep the family close like it was when mother was with us. This faded out too; it became too expensive to carry that load alone without everyone giving a fair amount of money to defray the cost of hosting food for a large family; especially when it included their kids and friends who would also come over to eat. As always, they left like everyone else without physically helping to clean up. Jean could not physically endure the long hours of work associated with preparing food for gatherings and for most holidays.

Although I love everyone still, I only feel close to my sister because we share and spend time together. When I see Tyler Perry's Family Reunion movies, I feel sad because we used to have that scenery first hand in our family. I cannot see that we will ever experience what we used to have, since Mother's departure.

I was depressed from medical conditions; the loss of my mother, the transition from military to civilian life with nowhere to turn that satisfied my innermost core. I wanted to conquer the world, but had no desire, no starting point and no plan. I missed my mother so much that I wanted to go with her, but I didn't have the nerve to commit suicide even though it crossed my mind. I knew God would not be pleased with me if I took my own life. What kind of Christian loses it under life's pressures? You could not look at me and tell, other than the weight gain, that I was a candidate for a mental breakdown. After retirement, instead of going to find work immediately like my husband did, I was in a daze most of the time. I stayed home and relaxed around the house and food became my best friend. I shot up over 200 pounds in no time. I had gained 30 pounds in one month when I came back from Korea. She was gone! I had retrieved some of my mom's clothes from my sister's shed prior to coming back to Washington State. They were dirty. I tried to find her smell. I was losing it slowly. I began to go the doctor often with more pain and an unstable mind set. I started experiencing dreams of having a stroke and heart attacks often. I physically felt the twitching and disfigure of my mouth, paralyzed on one side of my body, and I couldn't wake up after trying to become conscious. I would go the Emergency Room and share my experience with the doctors to see if the machines could trace the nightmares or physical problems. I started to believe that they were beginning to think I was crazy because I couldn't explain what was happening to me. I got mad at the doctors and my husband because no one seemed to believe me and my chronic pain had worsened.

Finally, I started to pray and ask God to save me from these disturbances because I could not convince anyone that I experienced these episodes. I was angry at the world and I remember feeling that someone, anyone owes me something because I retired from the United States Army. I needed to feel valued and wanted attention for doing very little. I needed a title and didn't know where it would come from nor could I strategize how to obtain one. I was in trouble because I felt as if I was exiting this world slowly in my mind and no one understood me. I wasn't that strong woman of God and leader that people saw in me. I became an introverted woman which did not set with me because I was the total opposite. I didn't know how to make the real Deborah come out. I fell down on my knees and prayed for God to help me snap out of it and ended up on the floor for hours. I felt God's presence all over me and my heart began to feel His words, "**You shall live and not die**". At that moment, I experienced total **peace that surpassed my understanding.** I got up to lie down on the bed and turned the TV on. I went to the CSPAN channel automatically and heard this middle age professor speak. I recall him talking about the world doesn't owe me anything and you have to pray that God expand your gifts and talents through education and hard work. He spoke about the disadvantages minorities have in America, but he also explained brilliantly that we have to pay attention and act. Success will not come to us; but we have to be in the right place at the right time. I jumped up and wrote down this man's name and stuck it somewhere. I felt as though God used this professors' message to confirm to me that if I take one step to improve my thinking, He will carry me to the next level.

Dr. West became one of my favorite professors. Months later, I attended an event at Evergreen State College in Olympia, Washington to hear this radical professor speak in person. I was pleased and entertained. Afterwards, people gathered around the stage to talk to him. It was noisy and I was about 10 feet and 20 people from him and saw that he was about to depart. I used my military voice (commanding tone) and called out Dr. West's name and proceed to tell him that God used him to speak to me on TV to get up and be liable for what I was already good at doing. I announced that I had recently retired from the ARMY. I said, "I had just come out into the real world, and you, Sir, encouraged me just by being you. Then I said, "Sir, thank you". Everything got quiet and everyone heard me along with the Doctor. He responded to me that he would never forget what I told him. He thanked me for sharing and wished me well. The look he gave me and the opportunity God allowed me to experience gave me a renewed charged.

I enrolled in Saint Martin University to finish up my degree in Psychology through a military program. I went back to my doctor for a Nutrition referral so I could learn how to eat healthier again. I got planted back into the church and started serving. My outlook and attitude were changing to everything good. The evil nightmares of becoming ill and dying departed from me. Satan had to release me from his grip of destruction. I mentioned Satan because the bible says his job is **to steal, kill and destroy** everything that will give our Lord and Savior Jesus Christ all the glory and praise for the blood that was shared on the cross for us to have the opportunity to have life and life more abundantly. When we call on that great Name, Jesus, and trust His word, we win. I prayed to God to send me a mother to love me. I needed somebody to act in this capacity in my life and I was not qualified to select this special person. I didn't want to mess it up because there was a need to get it right the first time. It had to be someone who would have the personal time to devote to me and be available for my kids on a personal level because they needed a grandmother too.

I went to a Nutrition appointment minding my own business. The class was almost over in about 15 to 20 minutes. Then, all of the sudden, I felt my heart palpitate. My first thought was Lord at least I am in the hospital for immediate assistance if I am experiencing a real heart attack. I remember thanking Him for me being in the right place for help. I felt God words in my heart saying, "that's her". I ask Him, "who!" "The lady sitting in front of you holding the cane," He said. He continued to say, "I choose her to be your mother". I asked God, "What do I say to her?" I felt His smile in my heart telling me since when had I been at a loss for words. I smiled back at Him! We were having a two way conversation in my heart. I felt God's Presence all over me. When I looked at the clock, we had 15 minutes left, and it seemed like one hour.

When she got up, I politely ask, "Madam, can I talk to you for a moment?" She was walking on her cane with a smooth glide and smiled at me and responded, "Why yes!" She had no idea what was about to happen. We got in the foyer area of Madigan Army Hospital. I introduced myself and so did she. I said these exact words. "God choose you to love me. I am retired military and don't want for nothing but love. I lost my mother and I prayed to God to send me somebody to love that will love me back and He chose you. Madam, I don't want anything from you because I have everything a woman could want. Therefore, all I need is your love and for you to accept mine. I am married and my husband and I are both retired military and we have two children." The lady I met, her name is Bennie Ruth Finley and she responded by saying, "Who me! God chose me! I've being praying for a young person to love!" She introduced me to her husband, Seth. We exchanged phone numbers. We went our separate ways for that day.

Later that night, I couldn't sleep. I tossed and turned and ask God to confirm what happened that day once more because it went so smooth. During this time, I was working out at Valley Fitness Center in Puyallup, Washington. The next morning, I was en-route to an exercising class and as I approach an intersection, I felt this strong urgency to call Mrs. Finley. I pulled over to a parking lot to talk. It was about 7:00 in the morning during a weekday. I had just dropped off our son to the daycare. When she answered the phone, she immediately said she was praying to God that if this is for real, have her call me! Then she asked me, "Are you for real?" I said, "Yes Ma'am, this is for real." She said, "I just prayed and the next moment, you called." I said, "WOW! I added, I had to stop what I was doing and call right away". I don't know what would have happened if I had not stopped and obeyed the prompting of the Holy Spirit to call Mrs. Finley. Without hesitation, she said, "You have to meet my family right away." She asks me if I would like to go out to dinner. I agreed to go. I met her sisters, her brother-in-law and her son. They are Auntie Annise, Auntie Clide, Auntie Gloria and Uncle Dewitt. Arcenia is her only son. He is retired from the Air Force. I call him, 'Brother Man.' There were also several other family members. I knew they needed to check me out to see if I was for real too. They looked me up and down to see what kind of woman I was; given that I was making contact with their senior sister. The dinner with her family was like sitting down with my biological family. I felt love and acceptance. But most of all, I felt the Presence of God. I was grateful to find out that we lived blocks apart up the road. I was like a little girl at Christmas. This was a huge gift that God gave me. I somehow felt complete. I now have this mother figure that was real and tangible.

God gave me another opportunity to show Mrs. Finley love as if she had birthed me. I never will, for the life of me, forget my real mother, but the loss and the void of motherly love were miraculously restored through the power of the Holy Spirit. Wow! What a blessing this family is to me. I call Mrs. Finley (the oldest sibling), Mom and it feels good. Seth became my Pops who took the time to talk to me like a caring and loving father. He was a World War II Veteran, and teacher who went home to be with our Lord. It has been 10 years of having her in my life. I call mom and her sisters, The Golden Girls because when I see them all together, they represent a strong tower for their large family. Women leaders, who are well respected and sought after when life gets tough and unmanageable, they are pillars that hold a family of siblings, cousins, uncles, aunts, grand and great grandchildren together as a single strong unit.

Mom and I departed Seattle, Washington for a Finley Family reunion in Michigan. I did not feel out of place. I am her daughter and it was unbelievably nourishing to my soul. I was grateful that my husband supported me when I wanted to travel with Mom for a week and escort her around town in style. My friend and walking partner, Mrs. Mildred Jonville kept our son, so I could go out of town and enjoy this outing with Mom. Mom is the same age as my mother, Lillie Bell Rivers. When I looked at Mom, I had a vision of my mother while we were in the hotel room. I had to call Auntie Annise to share that because it was an awesome experience. I feel love so strong in our friendship. I know God gave me a chance to experience a mother's love again.

No matter how lonely you may be, God can fill your voids too. Allow Him to do open heart surgery in your heart through His word and renew you mind by His word. I challenged you to trust in His word and listen with your heart. He will confirm His word and will be there for you. He has a way of putting you in the right place at the right time. What God has for you is for you and no one can stop Him if your trust Him with all your heart, mind and soul.

My Golden Girls are sisters.
They are mighty, impeccable and impactful Women of God.
Their leadership is respected and honored by family and friends.
They inspire me!

From Top Left to Right:
Reverend Clide Claudia Cobb, Gloria Jones,
Annise Curtis and Bennie Ruth Finley (my adopted mom)

Friendships

We need friends in our lives that we can trust to support us when need it. A friend is someone who is emotionally close; someone who we are fond of, and someone reliable. He or she is someone who will not always agree with you and tell you what you want to hear. A friend will roll up his or her sleeves of faith and stand with you when times are hard and celebrate with you when times are good. I had a friend who displayed overwhelming and overpowering love and assistance to the point of exhaustion. It ruined our relationship. I allowed it to progress for years because I never had any friends to care for me so deeply through love and actions. She had a personal relationship with my kids and was very close to my family. It was, at times, too good to be true even after 5 years of this experience. A neighbor had the keys to our home while we were on vacation. My friend went to our neighbors' house and asks for our keys because she wanted to drop off homemade soup and breads for us to eat after arriving home from vacation. During a telephone conversation, I gave our neighbor permission to allow my friend into our home and hung up the phone. I didn't think anything else about it other than how nice that was for my friend to do such a warm gesture for me and my family. I felt privileged to have someone so precious and caring.

While we were en route back home, I got a phone call hours later. My Asian neighbor ascent saying, "She don't come out!" I ask, WHO! She said, YOUR FRIEND! I had no idea what was specifically going on. I called my house and my friend answered the phone with excitement. She said, "Girlfriend, I cleaned your windows and kitchen, your junk drawer and spot cleaned your carpet too." I was in shock! I couldn't believe it! I remember saying to my husband that I believe that my friend is crazy. My husband said that that was your friend and she means well. I wasn't sure what to expect upon coming home. We pulled up in our driveway and my friend came out to greet us with open arms with hugs and kisses. She proceeded to show us the beautiful table display with breads and soups. She also showed me that she cleaned my windows and carpet. When she got to my junk drawer, it was nice, clean and neat. I did not receive this nice gesture very well at all. I asked my friend, where's my stuff?" My kitchen junk drawer was my personal space and I could always go and find something I needed whether I was looking for it or not. After this, I was uncomfortable with my friendship because we always talked about respecting personal space but it was getting worse. Each time I couldn't find something, I felt that my friend had it. I began to pray and ask God how I can get rid of a friend who loves me so much. I love her and I felt her love, but she didn't understand boundaries. This was the straw that broke the camels back in my tolerance. Meaning, I was beginning to evaluate whether I had peace around this friend. Did I trust her?

When I had situations with my daughter, she called my friend who gladly got involved. This was totally unacceptable! I addressed the issue with my friend to stay out of my personal life and she said that my daughter was 18 years old and she could talk to whomever she liked. My daughter was telling me that she was going to move in with my friend and her husband. I knew that I needed a change at this point. I no longer had peace around my friend, so I prayed and asked God to help me once again to dismantle this friendship. I didn't want to hurt her feelings because I felt in debt for all the love, attention and patience she had with me and my family. I answered my phone and door less and less frequently. And when she managed to catch me, I tried explaining boundaries for our friendship. She never displayed a clear understanding of how crucial adjustments to our friendship were needed. When we stopped communicating, something happened; it was a wonderful time of peace and serenity for me.

My stress levels remain high and intense until the friendship was physically dissolved. Today, I can love my friend from a distance with honor and respect. We talk on the phone about 3 to 4 times a year. I mentioned that one day we can be friends again in our senior years in God's timing. When God helps me with a friendship, I can love openly and freely; but when it is my entire plan, I mess everything up. When there is no peace around someone, you have to pay attention because it can affect your health, your family and your walk with God. Adjustments are necessary sometimes and that is not a negative thing to implement. It can make the difference between success and failure.

I continue to have friendships that I believe that God has put together. Recently, my husband and I went to California to see one of our friends and visit family. We discussed the task of writing what God had laid upon my heart years ago. Our families connected as if we had just seen one another yesterday. Our true love, respect and patience surfaced at first sight. We stayed a night with Marsha and her husband, Curtis and experienced royal treatment fit for a king and queen. We reminisced about old times, events, people and circumstances. We talked for hours. Although I was much larger in size then Marsha, I felt love and admiration for having the opportunity to see her again to express our love and friendship. I also have a friend who lives in Texas. Janice and Ronald is a one of a kind friend that will be with me forever. I know that we will love each other for the rest of our lives. I thank God for placing friends in my life that will be there for the long haul, and we don't have to see one another often nor do we need to talk daily, we just know the love is there to stay. When we finally see each other, it is as if we never missed a beat. Friends don't put you in bondage and they respect your feelings and space. I had to learn what true friendship was. If you experience no peace and seemed to be stressed when you are around people, check it out before it is too late. Make the necessary adjustments in your life so you can prosper and move in areas you desire.

I have also learned to discern real friendships and be in denial at the same time. There was a lady, who knew me when I first entered the military. I thought she was my friend until she threatened me in front of my family. She told me she was going to fuck me up. I was hurt, but not mad at her personally because God immediately surfaced in my heart telling me that I told you to get rid of her. My husband continued to drive us to our family outing and the truck was quiet. A short while later, my son, who was in the back seat of our SUV, asked me, "Mother, what does I'm goanna fuck you up mean? He was so innocent and concerned that a lady would say such a thing in front of my husband and child without any heart or remorse. My family has never seen me do anything but give my time and love to this lady. I explained to our son that no matter what you do for people, if they are jealous of you, they will mean you no good. So stay away and don't trust them. I further explained that the Holy Spirit has been warning me about this lady to dismiss her from my life. When you are blessed, someone will be jealous. And when people start to talk evil, the only option left is to remove them from your life. Otherwise, situations can get out of hand and someone can get hurt, which can change lives forever.

The strange thing about friendship is that God will lead and guide you to pick them up and leave them alone when the time comes. I ignored the voice of God on that particular friendship. I knew she was jealous of me, but I thought she loved me enough to get over it. I never did anything to try to stand out more than her because I was always giving of myself or anything I had. She often compared our lives on the tangible stuff we both possessed. I, it seemed to her, had it all. But, I am not materialistic and that is well known. I only need the basic essentials to live. Although our home is nice, I don't have a home that looks like a magazine on the inside. We use every room in our home and leave it messy sometimes until we get around to cleaning it up. I believe that we are a normal family who love one another and truly care about people.

Another friend in the military reminded me of how blessed I have been in being happy and enjoying my family. She shared how much she had been going through since we last heard from one another. I asked her if she were a believer. She shared that when we were on active duty, her son was kidnapped and God brought him back home to her safety. She lost him years later in a car accident. She told me that she almost died during childbirth with her daughter, and years later, lost her husband to illness. She explained to me that if she wasn't a believer depending on God, she would have lost her mind during these trying times.

There's an old saying, if you show me your friends, I'll show you yourself. I learn to draw a thin line on friendship. Sometimes, we can be so lonely from excluding God in our lives, that we allow people to leech on to us and suck us dry like a baby on a nipple for milk. We don't have to be on the phone everyday talking about others. We need to be on our knees talking to God about people and situations that we cannot change. He is the only one who can really and sincerely work it out without drama. The Holy Spirit will give you wisdom and words to say and what actions to take. You have to trust in Him with all your heart, mind and soul.

I am encouraging you to "Stand up woman of God! Stand up man of God! Be sturdy spiritually and be who God has created you to be." **Life and Death are in the power of the tongue.** You will have what you say you have. Evaluate your actions and conversations.

Faith comes by hearing and hearing the word of God. If you are hearing negative words that exalt themselves against the knowledge and truth of God, you are heading down the wrong path for your life. You cannot consistently entertain these negative words. I believe that God want us to be happy and healthy. **In Him we live, move and have our being**.

Would you trust Him today? Would you give your life to Christ today? Do you believe that God sent His Son, Jesus, to die on the cross for your sins and that Jesus is the Son of God? If you can confess this truth, then you are born again. Get with a believer that will steer you in the direction based on the word of God in Faith. Find a church that fits your spiritual growth needs. Most likely, there is a church in most neighborhoods 4 to 5 miles apart. If you do not have transportation, most churches have church buses that will pick you up and bring you back home. I challenge you to trust God for your life, no matter where you are now. I have had family members be delivered from drugs due to the power of prayer and action. I have been set free from gluttony through His grace and mercy and now I have will-power to eat healthier.

Parenting

God always sent someone to be there for us that we could trust to help us with our children while we both served in the military with unpredictable schedules. I knew from observing my mother that it was important to keep our kids in church, because that was the right thing to do. We hold them liable to make the best decisions possible for what they have been taught. We did not allow other kids to constantly hang out at our home, nor did we allow them to stay over-night with other people unless there was a structured and supervised event.

God allowed us to have two beautiful children to dedicate back to Him. I believe that we are responsible not only to nurture and raise our children, but we are liable to God for our kids' Spiritual growth first, as well as their academic education. We are being consistent in displaying protection for our children's future. God knows my concerns and He cares about all of them. Leamon, III is not allowed to fellowship with just any kid unless the child's parent(s) is actively involved with his or her son. Is it so easy for our kids to be in the wrong place at the wrong time? If kids don't obey their own parents, most likely they will rebel against my instructions too, which is not tolerated.

Being selective in choosing his friends is imperative until he gets older and mature enough to understand true friendship. It is easy to plan an event with another parent and this way, we will know what he is doing. We can only teach them to love and give back by setting that example. For instance, our daughter told me that she would have to take care of me when I get old because she saw my mother take care of my grandmother, her great-grand mother, and she was mean to my mother. My mother was an awesome lady to me with meekness I never understood back in the day.

There were times when my daughter called me 'mean' because she couldn't have her way. We are not our children's friends, but we are their parents. She wanted to go to a party that was over one of the teen's home at school. I made every attempt to meet the parents. After I got the address, I went over there a couple of days before this party and asked for either parent. According to the teen, neither of her parents was available so I left my home and cell phone numbers. I did not get a call from either of the parents. The night came for the party, Leamona asked again to attend this party. This was a nice home on a corner with plenty of land space. I refused to give in because something did not seem right. I would rather be safe than sorry. Leamona got over it and learned on the next school day that a trick was planned especially for her to experience that would have involved several other people.

As a mother, I could not afford to not trust my instincts because I knew I would respond in an unchristian way. We have to start discipline early in the life of our kids in order to gain enough value that we will not tolerate disrespect in our homes.

Our daughter did not hang out at the mall with her friends. However, when she got a job there, she had a reason to go to the mall: Work! She would often call me a 'Fun Sucker!' Although we did a lot together, there were times she was very hurt when I followed my heart on not allowing her to just roam freely with the girls. We don't apologize for our parenting style whether it was democratic or authoritative. Being flexible minded was crucial. When she wanted to run away, I ran to her room like a crazy woman and threw her suitcase at the door and told her to fill it up with whatever she wanted to take because that was all she was going to take with her. Our daughter thought, many times that I came down to whatever level was necessary in the most obscene way to get a point across to her. Really! I was acting most of the time. I don't know what I would have done if she had filled her suitcase and left. I didn't believe she had it in her to just leave because she couldn't have her way. Deep down, I was just acting like she was acting; fanatical! Maybe we both were in PMS syndrome at the same time. I always wanted that little girl to come out and play in order to make a point to Leamona. I was a teenage girl and have done almost everything under the sun. It is not safe now-a-days, but times are different now versus when I grew up.

It was necessary to educate our son at home using the Public On-Line School Option for starts. It has made a huge difference in our son's educational progress. Our son, Leamon, III started his education in a

Montessori school during pre-K and Kindergarten. First and second grade, he attended a local Christian private school. Bullying and other factors resulted in a school change. He attended a public school for 1 ½ months and I have been using Public On-line school option to obtain a quality education at our son's level. The traditional choice of sitting in a classroom no longer appeared to be the best choice for our son. Although it is a challenged at times, I have to pray and ask God to help me make the best decisions and sacrifices. Through our obedience, our son can succeed in every area of life. Our son is growing older and it was necessary to write a prayer for him to pray out loud daily before school. This prayer helps him hear God's Words in his prayer. It is specifically for him to grow and meditate on when no one else can help him understand all that little minds try to digest.

Our daughter was being bullied in Korea at her Elementary school. I told her that she better fight back and don't come back home complaining about other kids bothering her. She turned me in to her school counselor for giving her that advice. I was called to the school to explain myself. I stood my grounds that if the school staff couldn't control the situation, maybe I should talk to the parents of these kids. The parent was an officer and I was enlisted soldier. This situation got very sensitive, and I did not care about the rank structure in the military in this situation. The school staff decided to handle the student situation with their parents because I insisted on approaching these parents. The Lord knew that this was a cross-road for me when it came to our daughter. I never heard about problems again after that encounter with school staff.

When Leamona was in high school, she experienced bullying and decided that she would fight the girl who was harassing her. I was called to the principal's office to meet our daughter there. She met me in the hallway saying, "Mother, you are going to be so proud of me, I did it!" "I beat Cindy down because I have had enough" "You always wanted me to fight back, so I did." "Are you proud of me?" I asked Leamona to hold her voice down because this was not the time for a celebration of this accomplishment. Actually, I was a little embarrassed that she was so proud of fighting back. After all, it was her first fight ever! Right! It was close to exams time frame and I didn't want her to get expelled from school. I thought I would have to physically drive daily and pick up all her work, but by God's grace and mercy, she was allowed to test and go back home daily to complete semester testing. She was an honor student too.

As a mother, I did not always have the right answers or gave the best advice, but I noticed the difference in operating in wisdom verses ignorance when I don't stay prayed up. I followed my heart with God's help through His word, my Chaplains (Pastors), and friends. I had committed myself to set the best possible example that my mother set for me to live by. I will never be the woman she was, but I do have some of her qualities in trusting God to be the best woman of God I can be. I miss the mark when I don't pay attention. But, I learn quickly from my mistakes. I still have a lot to learn. I hardly have any secrets because I like to share what God is doing and has done in my life. This is why you are sharing a part of me now by reading this book.

During school days, in our home, we start our day with devotion whether it was a Boy Scout study guide of God and Me, God and Country or God and Church. It is imperative to teach my son to put God first. I believe that he will be a mighty man of God and he will be well-rounded spiritually, physically, academically and socially. We basically use the same parenting style of structure and supervision to ensure his child-hood is as safe as possible to experience the finest exposures and opportunities a young boy can have. He is soon to become a teenager. We talk about everything under the sun that's necessary. We are honest about teenage reasoning and the temporary 'know it all' outlook. I keep it real because I'm not a perfect mother, but a God fearing woman who will, at any odds, rise to whatever occasion possible in parenting to set the best Christian example.

I don't sugarcoat mistakes, but they are to be used as a lesson; not to make the same one over and over again. Yes, when something gets broken in our home by accident, it is okay because material things can be replaced but people are irreplaceable and should be treated with care. However, just as I have to watch what I am doing and pay attention, kids have to be taught that too. You cannot get mad and angry and ready to scold your kids every time something doesn't go right or gets broken around the house or anywhere else. We are all ways learning regardless of our age.

When young people are not taught to put God first, one day their world will change as they know it and they have to have something larger than life to hold onto for hope, restoration and edification. Jesus has been my answer to what ifs, what now, and Lord, I have messed up again! I call on His name quick to send me help and guidance before I make situations irreversible to repair.

If, you are facing trials and tribulations in a marriage relationship, pray hard and long about it before dismantling it. Don't give God a time table to work it out for you. Just know, He will work it out and give you wisdom to make the decision based on His word for your life. He often sends people your way to confirm that He heard or you may be flicking channels on your remote and end up on a TV station with an encouraging message that you were seeking from God. If you have a relationship with God, He will show you and protect you with signs and wonders. He will open and close doors necessary as you believe in Him to do what His will for your life as you **trust in Him with all your heart and lean not to your own understanding.** The bible is my parenting and relationship manual. We have to stay connected to His word so we don't misuse our parenting authority or abuse one another. It takes work, dedication and commitment constantly to live peacefully. It is worth every effort to make a relationship work for life. There are no perfect people; we all make mistakes intentionally or unintentionally.

I felt it was my personal responsibility to take care of our son's education, social schedule with other kids, sports participation decisions, etc. Between schooling, church, Boy Scouts, piano lessons, and bowling, I have to choose to believe that if we, as parents, do our best, the Holy Spirit will surely do the rest of the teaching and guiding our son as we are obedient to God as a couple. I had to teach our son the following prayer to recite daily to build his faith:

"I can do all things through Christ that strengthens me, I am above and not beneath, I will control my anger and have a great understanding. I will not have a hasty temper that causes me to make mistakes. Thank you Lord, for sending me Christian friends, and I will receive the desires of my heart through Jesus Christ. I am honorable, respectable and learning to live a Godly life with confidence. I trust God that I am smart and have

total recall of everything that I learn. Thank you Lord, I can read and speak clearly every time I open my mouth. I believe that God sent His son to die on the cross for me and God raise Him from the dead, and Jesus is God's only begotten Son. I am saved and I shall not be damned. Father, thank you for my parents, my sister, my dogs, Max and Charlie and everything you will do for me, in Jesus Name. Amen."

He prays this prayer that I wrote for him so he can hear himself say it daily as a start for his prayer life to build himself up by praying and believing that God can make a difference in his life too. It was necessary because of the negative influences he was receiving that started to have an impact on how he sees himself. I do believe that he will revise this prayer as he gets older. I saw a change in his life when he transitioned from the traditional educational system to the Public On-Line Schooling which allowed him to learn one on one at his pace without being left behind.

Submission

Sometimes submitting to Godly leadership is not easy when you have your own agenda and ideas about how things should be run. I had to learn that **obedience is better than sacrifice. If I love God with all my heart, mind and soul,** then everything I do is suppose to be done to His Glory, not mine whether I'm serving in a church atmosphere or anywhere else. If Church leaders are using the word of God to implement spiritual education based on His Word, and you attend or serve in that congregation, you are required by our Lord to submit to authority. What do I mean? Thanks for thinking of this question! Most of my life, I have been attending or serving in a military consolidated chapel system and rules have to be followed. Therefore, Pastors or Chaplains rotate their assignment every 2 to 3 years. Therefore, changes in operations are inevitable each time command positions change. I have experienced most chapels to be fully supported by military retirees whether they are Air Force, Army, Navy, Marines, and Department of Defense Employees. From Ushering to Hospitality to other committed Auxiliary positions to serve in, it is not a membership type congregation, but attendance and participation is open to any and all military affiliated personnel to plug in and grow as awesome families raising their kids and have their spiritual needs met at the same time.

I had to learn through making mistakes on how to be a productive leader for the Lord and allow God to adjust my attitude and disposition as often as it is was needed. I didn't always agree that I needed help in adjusting to changes and spiritual growth. It was not always easy to submit, but when I am reminded to salute and execute changes from my leaders, it was respecting not only their position, but honoring God to submit to leaders appointed over me. I can tell the difference in having peace in my atmosphere when I am doing right by God's word versus the turmoil in my heart when I don't honestly submit as the Spirit convicts me. This commotion spills over into my home life and professional life when I am not in good standing with the Lord. I cause problems with my family and friends by nit picking at everything and contributing to gossip. I hear the Holy Spirit speaking to my heart (in the back ground to stop it!), but, the fleshly part of me will keep going on and on because I have failed to feed my Spirit with the word of God. When I fall down; I can only get back up when I reconnect my heart to God and repent and come back to continue to serve and represent His goodness and Mercy in my life.

After retiring and returning to Joint Base Lewis McChord area, and shortly returning back to the Chapel services, I remembered, as a young woman, that the Women of the Chapel at the Old Chapel Nine were always available to talk with me, nurture me, and set an example for me to be a consistent woman of God. They encouraged me to just decide to live right and please God. The Grace Gospel Service on JBLM is almost 40 years old and some of the original members (men, women and families) are still attending, giving and serving this military community. These mighty women of God were still serving at the Chapel in a newer building doing the same thing; blessing young women to be **steadfast, unmovable, always abounding in the things of our Lord** no matter what happens in life. They are rare and seasoned women who I have grown to love and cherish for their willingness to love and serve through the good and bad times giving back to the military community. I know without a doubt that my life would not be the same without the influence of these strong military women of God. I submit to serve God while giving back to my inheritance of service in their senior years. I felt that the torch was passed to me and others to continue the tradition of military families serving God while supporting and serving one another. It was my time for leadership duties with the Pastors' blessing at that time whether it was Hospitality or Women's Ministry. It was so touching and emotional for me when I was asked to be our Women's Ministry Leader by one of my old active duty military friends named Mary and Mother Evans. I love these ladies amongst several others who support and trust God for our military families. The church mothers do keep me straight to this day when I seem to get to high or low.

My emotions ran high as I thought back at the years of military service while serving in military chapels, so I wrote a letter to the congregation and obtained permission by the current Pastor (at that time) to read prior to prayerfully assuming that responsibility:

I'm a Product of Women of the Chapel for the past 30+ years!

As a US Soldier on active duty, I was served and spiritually nurtured by Women of the Chapels at Fort Bragg, NC, Weis-botten, West Germany, Fort Lewis Chapel Nine and in Korea. I served in leadership positions in Protestant Women of the Chapel in Seoul Korea in 1989-1990, 1998-2000. I served and supported several Retreat Committees high on the Mountain Top in the middle of downtown Seoul Korea. And as a US Army Retiree, I have served with Grace Women of the Chapel, to Sisterhood (WOC) in 2009 which later was renamed Grace Women Ministry. I am honored and humbled to serve as your President. I trust to continue to have an outlet where ladies can come to a spiritual table and be fed the Word of God personally—while experiencing the love and support of other military women. These women include spouses, soldiers, widows, civilian employees, etc. We will all learn and grow together as mighty women of God. A place to relax, be renewed and be transformed among powerful and enriching times of teaching and worship with your fellow Sisters from all walks of life. Aspect catered meals, pot-lucks with fun, food and fellowship. Be prepared to escape the hustle bustle of our daily lives for monthly Bible study on the second Tuesday evenings; special holiday celebrations; our Annual Women's History Month program and the Mother Daughter Breakfast, Tea, Tunes and Testimonies, etc. This is where we can just be ourselves, dress up, and express that little girl in each of us. Women of the Chapel mission across America are adjusted to meet the needs of the current families attending our services. Come out and be a part of Women of the Chapel, submit your ideas, needs and desires to support one another. Sir, Thank for the opportunity to Serve, be led and lead our Women's Ministry.

I remember the day I read this letter and the comments I received afterwards. I knew that my history in serving in chapels was my destiny. I knew that conducting services for God had to be done in decently and in order no matter who was assigned the task of leading. Someone will always have negative and positive comments about everything, while they stand on the side lines watching the committed people who are willing to serve God in a church or to support events and activities. We have to keep focused on the high calling of Jesus Christ to serve whether it's a military chapel or civilian church.

It doesn't matter what church you go to, there are rules to follow. If you don't like rules, then sit down be quiet and listen and grow until you are ready to serve without complaining. If you need prayer, ask someone in authority or someone you trust to be a Godly man or woman to pray for you and with you while adding their faith with yours for God to move on your behalf. New believers in Christ get into a church quickly and get planted so you can grow into a strong tree. Your growth will take place through the watering of God's word in your heart and through spirit of fellowship. **Faith comes by hearing and hearing the word of God**. Therefore, you have to keep hearing it and think (meditate) on it and it will become part of your life. Also, there are excellent TV ministers to choose from until you find a church to go to that can assume the responsibility of your spiritual growth.

Don't worry about what who sings good, who wear unappealing clothes, who you like or dislike, or the size of the church congregation; just get God for yourself and watch Him change your thinking and your life. Then, you will have a heart to enhance the church's operations with what God has already instilled in you. **Many are called, but a few answer the calling of God on their life to serve.** There are no perfect churches where everything will be peaches and cream, therefore, go add your flavor and have fun learning and growing among believers. It is never too late to invite Jesus to be part of your life. You can trust Him with your finances and family 24 hours a day.

When you meet people and they share what they are going through, you will find the Holy Spirit will bring His words back to your remembrance when it's needed to share with them. Likewise, you will be blessed because you will **overcome what you are going through by the word of someone else's testimony**. Be careful on judging people's disposition because you will be judged just like you judged others, and when the shoe is on the other foot, it doesn't feel good, does it? You never know what people are going through.

Peace

We cannot give our own selves peace. When we are worried about something and don't see an answer, we are to pray to God because **He cares about everything that concerns us.** If you have problems in believing, get someone you trust who is a believer and have them add their faith with yours.

I knew my sister; Gloria Jean worked in food service almost 40 years with no medical coverage. She depended on God for everything. She loved cooking for different restaurants when she was able to work. She did the maximum of what she had to do while working and taking care of her kids. There were no programs on single parent education and childcare assistance. We assisted one another and had peace in God to sustain us. Our mother and grandmother (Lizzie Cross) were strong women who taught us to rely on God and do our best to take care of our home and family.

When Gloria's health started to decline, she relied on God to help her and medical care was available when it was needed, right on time. Yes, we serve and love an on time God. We talk about God every day. We believe in trusting Him for all we need and all we do, because we are nothing without Him. Down through the years, Jean always cooked large meals single handedly to keep the family together through fellowship. This became difficult, so it's time for everyone else to step up to the plate and be there for one another without leaving anyone out of the gatherings. Our mothers taught us to love.

The world is evil and you never know what to aspect from one moment to the next, but you can pray to God with a spirit of expectation that He will protect us from harm and danger and keep peace in our homes. We are human beings with different ideas and thoughts. We are all sinners and fall short of His Glory; therefore, we don't have to work for His grace and mercy. We just have to trust in Him with all our hearts through life's ups and downs. The things we can change, work hard to change them and the things we cannot change, we must trust Him.

This book has been my observations and experiences in the difference Jesus has made in being a part of my life. I was <u>never</u> told I will not amount to anything, but I was <u>never</u> told that I would amount to anything. I didn't feel sorry for myself because sometimes some things will happen out of our control. I had to strive and identify what success was for me and run with it. I could not compare myself with people who had more education or who had a lot more money or both than I did. No matter where you are in life, rich, poor, skinny, fat, lonely, etc., someone will be better or worse off at something than you. I know there are more beautiful women than myself with bigger houses, cars, more college graduated kids, etc. I never desired to live my life and keep up with the Jones per say. I just wanted God's grace and mercy to be there for me and my family because I knew that with Him, everything would be alright, regardless. Having His peace in my life was and still is priceless. I don't focus on who loves or hates me, because God will cause people to bless others regardless of how other people feel about them.

Father, bless the person who is reading this book now. Give them direction in the thickness of life's bushes. Lead them to the sword of your word to cut through turmoil, jealousy, hatred, anger, and to experience your peace for their lives. Put people around them so they will feel your love and presence. Lord, help them realize that they can do all things through You; if and when they choose to believe in God the Father, the Son and the Holy Spirit. **You are able to do exceedingly and abundantly above all they ask or think according the power that works in them.** Compel their hearts to surrender to Your will and Your way, and that they can come now just as they are to Your throne of Grace.

If you are a non believer and desire to accept Jesus Christ as your Lord and Savior, here is the sinner prayer for all of us:

I believe that God sent his son, Jesus Christ to die on the cross for my sins and Jesus Christ is my Lord and Savior and I ask You to come into my heart and saved me from my sins.

This is all that is required to be saved! You most likely will not hear thunder bolts, but the Angels in Heaven will be rejoicing for your decision.

Virginia Mathews

Creative Designs in Graphics and Event Planning

My book cover is special. The cross and ribbon represents Jesus dying on the cross for our sins, the sun is a reflection of His true light that shines in darkness, the shield is a symbol of having the breast plate of rightness to guard our hearts, the sky reminds me of the heavens above, the butterfly is a reflections of me living to get to heaven with Christ, and the sword inside reminds me that Gods' word is **Sharper than any double-edged sword, it penetrates even to dividing soul and spirit, joints and marrow; it judges the thoughts and attitudes of the heart.**

Finally, the title, without Christ, I am nobody, but with Him,
I am beautifully and wonderfully made in His image.

Leamona Renee Woodley
I love her dearly

Graduated from Alabama State University and
she enjoy beaches around the world.
Zeta Phi Beta, Sorority, Inc.

She is definitely her own woman who is learning to operate in what
she wants out of life. Leamona is talented and a hard worker. I enjoy
having her as my daughter. I am proud of her and support her in all
her endeavors. She is smart and responsible

Go Leamona!

You're the Best!

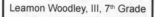
Leamon Woodley, III, 7th Grade

I choose to trust God for our son's destiny. He is a mighty man of God in the making and we will continue to expose him to the best exposures possible. Being well rounded is the key to a diverse and happy life. God made the world for us to enjoy and be all we can be and give Him all the Glory. Currently he is a First Class Boy Scout of America, and he enjoys the outdoors along with fishing, hiking, snow-shoeing, etc. My prayer for him is to make a difference in society that will please God and enjoy what he chooses to do that will allow him to live a productive life.

Leamon Woodley, Jr.
Washington State Power-Lifting Hall of Fame:
March 5, 2011

At 54 years old, Leamon Woodley is in better physical condition than many Soldiers half his age.

The retired Master Sergeant competed in the 2011 Washington State Powerlifting Bench Press and Deadlift Championship.

Woodley set two national records, including the squat at 640 pounds and total weight at 1,654 pounds.

References

Bold phase print in my writings were scriptures paraphrased

My Bible Versions: Life Application, Kings James, and the Living Bible

Proverbs 18:22   **The man who finds a wife finds a good thing; she is a blessing to him from the Lord.**

Philippians 4:13   **I can all things through Christ who strengthens me**

2 Corinthians 10:5   **Take captured of every thought that exhaust itself against the word of God.**

2 Corinthians 5:7   **Walk by faith and not by sight**

Mathew 19:26   **All things are possible to them that believe**

Proverbs 18:21   **Life and death is in the power of the tongue**

1 Corinthians 4:5   **Everything done in darkness shall come to light.**

Deuteronomy 31:6   **He said, "I will never leave you nor forsake you"**

Proverbs 17:22   **Cheerful heart is medicine and a broken spirit makes one sick.**

Psalm 55:22   **Cast your cares on the LORD and he will sustain you; he will never let the righteous be shaken.**

Philippians 4:4-7   **Peace that surpassed my understanding**

Romans 10:17	Faith comes by hearing and hearing the word of God
Acts 17:28	In Him we move and have our being
Ephesians 3:20	Now to Him who is able to do exceedingly abundantly above all that we ask or think, according to the power that works in us
John 3:16	For God so loved the world that he gave his one and only Son, that whoever believes in him shall not perish but have eternal life.
Hebrews 4:12	For the word of God is alive and active. Sharper than any double-edged sword, it penetrates even to dividing soul and spirit, joints and marrow; it judges the thoughts and attitudes of the heart.

Editing Credits

"Deborah Woodley invites you to join her in a song of praise to the Almighty. Her personal narrative is a testimony to an essential belief that she holds dear: 'let everything that has breath, praise the Lord.' She begins in her youth and lays out for you how she experienced the benefits of having a good mother. In spite of many difficulties, her mother never allowed the negative situations in her life to get the best of her. Her mother was a woman of faith, who taught her children the importance of remembering God and knowing that God is an ever present help in the time of trouble. Woodley's narrative is not the biography of a brigadier general. But, it is the story of a woman who traversed the challenges of being a female in the military; yet maintain a peace filled life because she trusted in the sovereignty of God. Her faith advances her to the rank of 'Five Star General' in the spirit. From the first page to the last page, you encounter a woman of God, who knows the difference that having a relationship with God has made. She is a seasoned saint, whose love for God has stood the test of time. She remains committed to her Lord and Savior and invites you to get to know Him and to love Him as she does. He has been a powerful force in her life and met every need that she has had. She clearly tells you, that God will fill every void in your life and meet your every need, if you will only trust Him. Her life tells you that He will truly make a way out of no way."

Deborah C. Umrani, Ph.D.
Assistant Professor
University of Illinois at Chicago
College of Education

Author Biography

Born and raised in Chattanooga, Tennessee by the late and great Lillie Bell Rivers, and is youngest of six siblings. Graduated from Brainerd High School in 1979 and entered active duty to serve her country at age 17. Deborah Woodley is the wife of Leamon Woodley, Jr. of 30 years with two beautiful children. Along with her husband, she is a United States Army Retiree of 21 years. She earned a Bachelor's Degree in Psychology: with a minor in Sociology. She has experienced as a Washington State Registered Counselor, Certified Parenting Instructor and Home Care Provider. She is an outstanding Christian Leader who sets the example in serving and loving people of all walks of life without compromising. She has served in many areas across the globe to include West Germany and Belgium in Europe, Republic of Seoul Korea in Asia, Anchorage Alaska, Fort Bragg, North Carolina, Joint Base Lewis McChord, Washington, and has travel to Paris France, Sweden, Mallorca Spain, Virgin Islands, Bahamas and several states across America. Mrs. Woodley is a devoted mother and solid friend to her sister Gloria Jean Hill and many more people who trust God for everything. Along with being a Home-maker and Educational Advocate for her son, she is grateful to God for her family in being a driven force of priority and completeness. She values K12 On-Line School Learning for educating her son Leamon III for the past 4 years, and actively supports him in his tenure in the Boy Scout of America progress and success for the past 7 years. She is a proud mother of her adult daughter Leamona who is the first grand-child of Mrs. Rivers to be a college graduate (Alabama State University with a major in Communication and Public Relations).